T0286950

Cambridge Elements ≡

Elements in Quantitative and Computational Methods for the
Social Sciences
edited by
R. Michael Alvarez
California Institute of Technology
Nathaniel Beck
New York University

USING SHINY TO TEACH ECONOMETRIC MODELS

Shawna K. Metzger
University of Virginia

CAMBRIDGE
UNIVERSITY PRESS

CAMBRIDGE
UNIVERSITY PRESS

University Printing House, Cambridge CB2 8BS, United Kingdom

One Liberty Plaza, 20th Floor, New York, NY 10006, USA

477 Williamstown Road, Port Melbourne, VIC 3207, Australia

314–321, 3rd Floor, Plot 3, Splendor Forum, Jasola District Centre,
New Delhi – 110025, India

79 Anson Road, #06–04/06, Singapore 079906

Cambridge University Press is part of the University of Cambridge.

It furthers the University's mission by disseminating knowledge in the pursuit of
education, learning, and research at the highest international levels of excellence.

www.cambridge.org
Information on this title: www.cambridge.org/9781108793407
DOI: 10.1017/9781108883993

© Shawna K. Metzger 2021

This publication is in copyright. Subject to statutory exception
and to the provisions of relevant collective licensing agreements,
no reproduction of any part may take place without the written
permission of Cambridge University Press.

First published 2021

A catalogue record for this publication is available from the British Library.

ISBN 978-1-108-79340-7 Paperback
ISSN 2398-4023 (online)
ISSN 2514-3794 (print)

Additional resources for this publication at www.cambridge.org/metzger

Cambridge University Press has no responsibility for the persistence or accuracy of
URLs for external or third-party internet websites referred to in this publication
and does not guarantee that any content on such websites is, or will remain,
accurate or appropriate.

Using Shiny to Teach Econometric Models

Elements in Quantitative and Computational Methods for the Social Sciences

DOI: 10.1017/9781108883993
First published online: April 2021

Shawna K. Metzger
University of Virginia

Author for correspondence: Shawna K. Metzger, skmetzger@virginia.edu

Abstract: This Element discusses how Shiny, an R package, can help instructors teach quantitative methods more effectively by way of interactive web apps. The interactivity increases instructors' effectiveness by making students more active participants in the learning process, allowing them to engage with otherwise complex material in an accessible, dynamic way. The Element offers four detailed apps that cover two fundamental linear regression topics: estimation methods (least squares, maximum likelihood) and the classic linear regression assumptions. It includes a summary of what the apps can be used to demonstrate, detailed descriptions of the apps' full capabilities, vignettes from actual class use, and example activities. Two other apps pertain to a more advanced topic (LASSO), with similar supporting material. For instructors interested in modifying the apps, the Element also documents the main apps' general code structure, highlights some of the more likely modifications, and goes through what functions need to be amended.

Keywords: Shiny, teaching, web apps, quantitative methods, regression

© Shawna K. Metzger 2021

ISBNs: 9781108793407 (PB), 9781108883993 (OC)
ISSNs: 2398-4023 (online), 2514-3794 (print)

Contents

Locations for Element's Shiny Apps

CO https://doi.org/10.24433/CO.2852743.v1

○ https://github.com/MetzgerSK/shinyElement
(houses all the Binder links/Binder usage notes)

The GitHub repo and Code Ocean capsule are
functionally identical (see fn. 1).

Full URLs for any app: https://mybinder.org/v2/gh/MetzgerSK/shiny
Element/major?urlpath=shiny/*appName*/, where *appName* corresponds to the
name of the app.

To launch any of the apps instantly via Binder using the shortened URLs:

2: Modifying the Apps
- whySurv: https://bit.ly/3oqe9WM
- mleLogit: https://bit.ly/348YW5F

3: Defining "Best": Estimation
- leastSq: https://bit.ly/347SCeL
- mleLM: https://bit.ly/39fDWe1

4: Linear Model Assumptions
- olsApp: https://bit.ly/33IXQN5
- linRegEstms: https://bit.ly/2YCij3g

5: Encore: Shrinkage Methods
- leastSqLASSO: https://bit.ly/37u2b7C
- LASSO_bchamp: Code Ocean capsule only (file sizes too big)
- LASSO_bchamp_lite: https://bit.ly/39IQFs0

B: Writing a Basic App: Predicted Quantities
- predProbs: https://bit.ly/2OXScSR
- predProbs 2.0: http://bit.ly/2CB4smh
- predProbs_HMST: https://bit.ly/3vK6BCN
- predProbsMNL: http://bit.ly/3g8o4fb

1 Introduction

Using Shiny to Teach Econometric Models focuses on how instructors can teach econometrics more effectively (and efficiently) to their students using Shiny apps. It does so by offering four multifaceted apps that focus on two fundamental ideas in econometrics: (1) defining what a best-fit line is and (2) how well we can estimate this line's equation under a number of conditions, if we have an interest in generalizing our findings back to a larger population. Further, it offers two additional apps pertaining to LASSO models to show Shiny's abilities to help students engage with more advanced topics. Across all six apps, the Element offers sets of example activities involving them. The apps' full capabilities and example activities are broadly written for a first-year PhD seminar in linear regression or an advanced upper-level undergraduate econometrics course, but others may find pieces of it useful for additional courses as well.

shiny is an R package written by Joe Cheng of RStudio that provides functionality to produce interactive interfaces or displays. As the blog post announcing the package's public beta in November 2012 says:

> Shiny makes it super simple for R users to turn analyses into interactive web applications that anyone can use. These applications let you specify input parameters using friendly controls like sliders, drop-downs, and text fields; and they can easily incorporate any number of outputs like plots, tables, and summaries.
>
> No HTML or JavaScript knowledge is necessary. If you have some experience with R, you're just minutes away from combining the statistical power of R with the simplicity of a web page.

> https://blog.rstudio.com/2012/11/08/introducing-shiny/

Throughout the Element, I use "shiny" to refer to the specific R package and "Shiny" to refer to the apps you can write using the package's functionality. I also use the phrase "regular R" to refer to conventional, non-Shiny R code.

1.1 Why Is Shiny Helpful for Teaching Econometrics?

To get a sense of why Shiny is helpful for teaching econometrics, it helps to understand what Shiny can do. Simply put, for an overwhelming number of things (if not nearly all), Shiny can do anything R can. It can also do more than R, which is where its power lies. Shiny can dynamically display text, Console output from R commands, LaTeX equations, interactive and sortable data tables, images, videos, static or interactive graphs, network diagrams, or interactive maps. Additionally, Shiny apps can accept user input through sliders, radio buttons, checkboxes, dropdowns, text input, toggle buttons, and file uploads, including "uploads" of R objects already in memory.

The Element's apps center around Shiny's ability to take various interactive inputs from the user, perform any number of tasks, and then output information involving the inputs. These outputs are *dynamic* – their contents will update in real time if users make changes to the app's inputs. This dynamic, interactive aspect distinguishes Shiny from other ways of doing things in R. The same dynamicism provides students with an easy way of exploring content that is impossible to do with regular R code.

The four main apps in this Element provide two thematic examples of Shiny's abilities:

1. Shiny gives students a way to *make otherwise abstract mathematical expressions concrete*. Our examples will involve mathematical functions. Shiny gives students the ability to *see* what these functions look like and how a function's output responds to changes in its key parameters, providing an enhanced foundation for discussing more complex concepts involving the functions. The Element's apps exploit this functionality to show students what we mean when we say a regression model is estimated with "least squares" or "maximum likelihood" (Section 3). The Shiny apps in this section prompt students to manually find the best regression estimates for a set of data, for each type of estimation (`leastSq` and `mleLM`, respectively). One of the two advanced-topic apps in Section 5, `leastSqLASSO`, does the same in a LASSO context.

2. Shiny provides an easier way to *execute simulations* of all kinds. Our focus will be Monte Carlo simulations (Section 4). These Shiny apps automate our simulation runs, allowing us to direct our students' focus to what the simulations substantively assess, and what the results show in that regard. One of the Element's apps uses Shiny to see how OLS performs under various conditions, with students being able to choose those conditions interactively (`olsApp`). The other app compares OLS's performance to other, common estimators under the same conditions as `olsApp` (`linRegEstms`).

The sixth and final app takes an applied article about LASSO, converts one of its replication files into app form, and allows students to try out myriad model specifications. They can then draw conclusions about which model is "best," given the article's professed aim (Section 5).

Shiny has the added bonus of being R-based – a language with which many social scientists are already familiar. Should you want to modify any of the Element's apps, you are in a position to do so. Section 2 talks about the apps' inner workings, laying out their logic, pointing out the major ways in which you might want to tweak them, and making note of what you would need to change to do so.

1.2 Why Is This New?

The idea of teaching statistics using interactive apps is not new. Rice University's Virtual Lab in Statistics,[1] Lock et al.'s StatKey,[2] Brown University's Seeing Theory,[3] and Math is Fun[4] are all examples of this tradition, with some of the apps going back to the 1990s. However, most statistics apps have traditionally focused on basic statistical concepts, such as sampling distributions and the Central Limit Theorem, statistical power, *t*-tests, and bivariate correlation. All of these concepts merit such attention because they lay important foundations for the more advanced discussions in later coursework.

Yet, detailed apps pertaining to these more advanced topics are rarer. The later topics' complexity makes them prime candidates for apps, in part because apps can provide guided, constructive, low-stakes ways for students to explore a topic. Pre-class activities using the apps can prime students to key in to certain words and phrases as they read and during lecture. In-class activities can help concretize (or, in some cases, motivate future) class discussions. This Element takes the first step in addressing this shortage by providing apps that focus on basic estimation techniques and linear regression.

In the ideal, the apps can allow you to teach the same content in less time than usual. This is a powerful potential efficiency gain, especially when methods courses are typically expected to cover much ground in a limited amount of time. The apps show one way to get "fundamental concepts [to be] accessible" to students, while "minimiz[ing] prerequisites to research" – a practice that some argue undergraduate math and statistics courses should adopt, with some social scientists advocating similarly for our methods courses. The Element does this by:

- Providing a conceptual overview of the major points each app can demonstrate at the beginning of each app section, along with a discussion of how I specifically use the apps when I teach that topic
- Discussing each app's specific features in more detail, in a research design-like flavor
- Providing 3–5 example activities for each section that can be tailored more specifically to fulfill your learning outcomes

---

[1] http://onlinestatbook.com/stat_sim/index.html
[2] http://www.lock5stat.com/StatKey/index.html
[3] https://seeing-theory.brown.edu/
[4] https://www.mathsisfun.com/data/index.html

- Laying out the broad strokes of the apps' inner workings in a separate section (Section 2), should you want to modify the apps for your own purposes, as I mentioned earlier

In this sense, the Element falls under the same header as Gelman and Nolan's *Teaching Statistics: A Bag of Tricks* (2017), where the authors discuss various demonstrations and examples for teaching quantitative material.

1.3 Pedagogical Motivations and Use

Appreciable research already exists on effective teaching strategies for mathematics and statistics. Reviewing it all is not this Element's purpose; Groth (2013, particularly chs. 1–2) provides a nice overview of the literature's broad evolution and major findings. A recurring meta-theme is that no one-size-fits-all approach to teaching exists. The notion of "healthy living" provides a useful analog (quoted in Groth 2013, 29):

> Health professionals have promoted the goal of a healthful life for years and have conducted a great deal of research but are still unable to specify the best way of meeting that goal. Exactly how much exercise do we need? Are seven servings of fruits and vegetables each day required, or would five be enough? What is your optimal weight? Our bodies are too complicated to specify the best path to a healthful life. The same is true in mathematics education. Teachers cannot expect to get clear and specific answers from research for exactly which textbooks or activities to use.
>
> *J. Hiebert, "What can we expect from research?" (2000, 168)*

Depending on the institution, instructor, level of instruction, topic, learning outcomes, and students, what works in one class will not necessarily work well in others. Being cognizant of this fact is half the battle.

The particular set of guiding principles behind this Element's contents stem from my own experiences with the confluence of these factors, as well as some of the broader arguments from the pedagogical literature regarding learning, critical thinking, and quantitative knowledge. Four such guiding principles motivated how and why I constructed the apps and their corresponding example activities:

1. Students learn material better when they are *active* participants (Biggs and Tang, 2011).
   > COROLLARY: Structure (some) tasks and activities such that the students work through the problems themselves in small methodical steps, rather than being led, told, or being expected to make large conceptual leaps on their own.

2. Prompting students to *reflect* on their knowledge ("metacognition") helps them to consolidate it (Yancey, 2009). Reflection can range from an informal sentence or two describing a pattern or explaining a connection to a more formal written assessment.

  ❯ COROLLARY: Using *writing to learn* (i.e., as a means), instead of only using it to demonstrate knowledge (as an end), can help facilitate this process (Menary, 2007), even in quantitative contexts (Bahls, 2012).

3. Part of consolidating knowledge involves encouraging students to make connections across topics within and across courses ("integrative learning") (Yancey, 2009), raising the chance they will be able to recall the information correctly later, even in new contexts.

4. From a quantitative angle, *multiple modes* of representation increase students' probability of grasping a problem or method (Box 1.1, sometimes also called the "rule of four" or part of the "Harvard calculus curriculum") (National Council of Teachers of Mathematics, 2000).

Box 1.1 Rule of Four: Multiple Representations

1. Descriptively (verbal explanations, written explanations)
2. Algebraic (symbolically, like equations)
3. Graphical (pictures, graphs, diagrams)
4. Numerical (actual data, other worked examples with actual numbers inserted)

As examples of how the apps and activities speak to these four principles, they:

1. Provide a way for students to explore key ideas on their own, but in a structured, sequenced environment.

  ❯ E.g., for an informal activity, telling students "This app demonstrates the effect of omitting a key covariate. [*Implying the requisite evidence is already present; students do not have to figure out what calculations to run.*] What happens to our estimates?"

2. Giving students further opportunities to explore in a less structured environment.

  ❯ E.g., being able to download a fake dataset with known assumption violations to analyze in R or Stata.

3. Explicitly ask students where key concepts appear in the apps; and then (if relevant) further prompting them to think about variants of those concepts, and how said variants would manifest, given the app's depiction of the parent concept.

❯ E.g., for a more formal activity, "What's the effect of omitting a key covariate? How does that tie to a sampling distribution? What pieces (if any) of the app speak to sampling distributions? What evidence should you see, given the effect you noted? What would the absence of such evidence look like?"

4. Focusing on a set of concepts or ideas in different contexts

❯ E.g., for the linear regression apps, always having available all the major residual diagnostic plots, regardless of the assumption violation under examination

5. Use as many modes of representation as possible to illustrate an app's key idea(s), if not all four modes

❯ E.g., the estimation method apps have a ❓ What's going on here? button whose pop-up box explains what the app does (*description*); they show the generic expression for the app's definition of best fit (via pop-up box) (*algebraic*); they plot the fake data (*x* vs. *y*) with the proposed best-fit line superimposed (*graphical*); and they print out the actual data values + the proposed parameter values inserted into the best-fit expression (among other things) (*numeric*)

How I use the apps in my own teaching varies. Generally, my usage falls into one of two categories:

1. A *pre-class activity* with two or three informal questions for students to think through as they interact with an app, but very little contextual information otherwise. The idea is to give students low-stakes exposure to the upcoming lecture's key ideas in a situation that fosters developing their intuition about said ideas before formalizing them. I then start the lecture by asking students what the app seems to do and letting the discussion grow organically from there. The discussion then parlays into the lecture proper, where I make a point of drawing explicit links between the app's output and the new content we just discussed. For in-class activities whose questions are a bit more formalized, I tell students to spend no more than 25–30 minutes on them.

2. An *in-class activity*, where I make some brief introductory remarks before breaking students into pairs or triplets (depending on the app + its associated activity) and explain the activity, usually via a worksheet. The activity usually goes for 10–20 minutes, depending on the quality of the side conversations I overhear as I circulate around the room. After the activity concludes and we reassemble as a class, the lecture continues as normal, with one difference: when we hit key ideas illustrated by the app, I say as much outright

before asking students to describe the patterns they observed from the relevant part of the activity (e.g., for the simulation apps, whether the estimates were biased for a particular violation and what led them to their conclusion).

I briefly outline how I use the various apps at the start of each section, for concrete examples. In general, I determine whether and how to use the apps on a topic-by-topic basis, first figuring out what three to five takeaway points I want the students to understand. From there, I work backwards to figure out what constituting pieces of knowledge they need to reach those points. I then think about whether and when students have seen these various pieces and start making decisions about whether a pre-class or in-class activity (or both) makes sense, what the activities' purpose should be, and therefore what they should look like. Finally, I decide whether an app makes sense (and if so, what the app would look like).

Regardless of whether the activity is pre-class or in class, there is an important commonality. Students need to *see and learn* how the various pieces of information are connected in the context of a specific topic or concept before they can begin consolidating their knowledge. Part of my role as the instructor is to help facilitate these connections by pointing them out explicitly, if not also taking a step back to discuss *how* students might have made these connections on their own, to raise the probability of students making them organically in the future.

1.4 Practicalities: Teaching Logistics

If you decide to incorporate Shiny into your teaching, there are two logistical issues you will need to address:

1. Deciding how to make the app available for students to use (Sect. 1.4.1)
2. Telling students how to access the app (Sect. 1.4.2)

1.4.1 App Availability

All of the Element's apps can already be run by students without further setup on your part using Binder, a service that runs GitHub repositories in one-off R sessions.[5] The GitHub repo and its apps are already configured to run in

---

[5] The Element's GitHub repo and its Code Ocean capsule of record are functionally identical as of this writing. The GitHub code is written for Binder, which currently uses R 3.6.3 (vs. the Code Ocean code [R 4.0]). The different R versions only matter in two small instances: (1) mleLM's server.R, when estimating the model, and (2) LASSO_bchamp_lite's server.R, when initializing the coefRes object. Over time, there may be tweaks to the GitHub code, which the repo's commit history will make evident, but the Code Ocean capsule's code will remain the same.

Binder; users only need the URL to access them (see Section 1.4.2). For one of the apps, only a simpler version is runnable using Binder because of Git's file size limitations (LASSO_bchamp). The full version runs in the Code Ocean capsule without issue.

There are several other ways to make Shiny apps accessible to students, as Appendix A.1 discusses further. Each option has strengths and weaknesses. Suffice it to say, Binder has the fewest drawbacks for this Element's purposes.

1.4.2 Access Instructions

Users access a Binder (= an app) by entering its URL into a web browser. The app Binders anywhere from 10–60 seconds to load. The Binder URLs for this Element's apps are listed in several places:

- At the bottom of the Element's GitHub repo (either the actual repo[6] or the streamlined version[7] – the page's contents are identical)
- In the "App Overview" segments that open Sections 3–5
- The beginning of the subsection in which the app is discussed in detail

There are a few ways to share the Binder URLs with students. Possibilities include:

1. Giving them the GitHub repository's URL,[8] the name of the app you want them to access, and tell them to click `launch binder` next to the app's name
2. The same as the previous point, except giving them the URL for the stream-lined, but otherwise identical[9] page that moves the readme first and hides the GitHub repo's file structure
3. Emailing them the link or pasting it into a slide at the end of the preceding lecture's PowerPoint, shortening the link as needed (e.g., using bit.ly[10])
4. If you know in advance that you will be incorporating an app into a particular lecture: shortening the Binder URL and including it in the syllabus under the assigned readings for that lecture (e.g., for mleLM: https://bit.ly/39fDWe1)

1.5 Element's Outline

Not including this introduction, the Element is organized into five sections. The next section discusses how to modify the Shiny apps (Section 2). You can skip it without consequence if you have no interest in doing so.

6[6] https://github.com/MetzgerSK/shinyElement
[7] https://MetzgerSK.github.io/shinyElement
[8] https://github.com/MetzgerSK/shinyElement
[9] https://MetzgerSK.github.io/shinyElement
[10] http://bit.ly

Sections 3 and 4 are the principal sections, each focusing on two apps. Section 5 contains the two other apps on a more advanced topic (LASSO).

The layout for each of these three sections is similar:

- **App Overview**: brief descriptions of the apps appearing in the section, along with repeats of the apps' Binder links.
- **Introductory Remarks**: situating the apps' general topic and motivation. For the two principal sections, I also discuss how I use the apps in my own teaching in this segment.
- **Major Points**: a list of points that the section's apps can be used to demonstrate. The lists are not exhaustive, but are meant to serve as a quick overview of some of the proverbial punchlines. The points are also meant to help you populate some possible activity ideas beyond the Element's examples, as your intended learning outcomes may be different than the ones from the illustrative activities.
- **App-Specific Segments**: methodically goes through each of the app's tabs in more detail to discuss the app's features – the means corresponding to the "Major Point" segment's ends.
- **Example Activities**: a small set of activities involving the apps, to help illustrate how the apps can be integrated into a course. The activities for each section correspond to a loosely articulated set of intended learning outcomes. For that reason, they may not suit for all, but should give you some ideas about how the apps can be used.

The sixth and final section provides some brief concluding remarks.

2 Modifying the Apps

If you have no interest in modifying the Element's apps for your own ends, you can safely skip this entire section. It goes into various technical details about the apps, but understanding the apps' details is not necessary to use them.

Many tutorials already exist about writing Shiny apps. Appendix B.2 contains a list of the basic introductory material. Appendix B also contains a walkthrough for constructing a full app specific to econometrics, highlighting several features particularly useful in that context.

Rather than cover well-trodden ground, this section instead details the basic structure of this Element's major apps. As I mentioned earlier, the apps cluster into two major categories: those involving *estimation methods* and those involving *simulations*. Regardless of type, all apps within a cluster have the same general code structure, meaning a simple grasp of that structure makes

Table 2.1 Simulation apps, quick reference table

	New	Existing
	Adding	*Modifying*
Page, in general	p. 19	p. 20
Subpage, in general	p. 19	p. 20
DGP	p. 14 (`server.R`) p. 22 (`ui.R`)	p. 14
Model	p. 16 (`server.R`) p. 22 (`ui.R`)	p. 16
Graph/table	p. 17 (`server.R`) p. 22 (`ui.R`)	p. 16
Displayed equation	p. 18	p. 18

it possible for others to more easily extend or otherwise modify an app for additional situations.

I spend most of the time discussing the simulation-based apps, as they are the more complex of the two clusters. Sketching out these apps' broad parts also covers a fair bit of ground, enough that I discuss them first, then the estimation methods apps second. The discussion assumes basic familiarity with shiny's terminology, programming concepts, and syntax.

This section does not have formal apps as such, but I mention two that do not appear elsewhere in the Element:

- whySurv [https://bit.ly/3oqe9WM]
- mleLogit [https://bit.ly/348YW5F]

2.1 Simulation Apps (olsApp, linRegEstms)

Table 2.1 provides a quick reference list containing some likely modifications for the simulation apps and the corresponding page numbers where I discuss them, should you know what you want to add or modify. I use the whySurv app as this subsection's running example (Fig. 2.1). The app examines two of the reasons why ordinary least squares (OLS) can perform poorly when the dependent variable is some length of time (i.e., a duration). It uses simulations to juxtapose OLS's performance with models better equipped to address duration data. whySurv has the same structure as Section 4's two

Figure 2.1 whySurv, "Right Censoring" tab after running simulations.
Package version: shiny_1.4.0.2

simulation apps, including the same three core tabs: "Main," "Raw Simulation Output," and "Distribution Graph" (labeled "Estimates: Distribution Plots" in the other apps). Unlike the Element's two official simulation apps, though, whySurv has few extra embellishments (on purpose), making it a good demonstration case.

2.1.1 server.R

If you want to add any functionality to an app, you will have to edit server.R, which defines all the backend R calculations. Informally, server.R holds the code that would appear in a regular R file, were this not a Shiny app: data wrangling, model estimating, graph creating,

table generating, text printing, data saving, and so on. With few exceptions, all calculations must be carried out in server.R. This is *always* true
for all calculations involving information entered by the user, like widget
values.

The general structure for the simulation code comes from Francis Smart.[11]
The virtue of Smart's code is that we can easily add additional data generating
processes (DGPs) or estimated models without massive rewrites. The code has
three basic parts:

1. A function that runs the simulations (MC_easy())
2. A function that generates one dataset from a user-defined DGP
   (OLS_data())
3. A function that specifies the model to estimate on a sampled dataset
   (OLS_est())

A simplified, lightly modified version of it also appears below:

——————————————— **Smart's original code (simplified)** ———————————————

```
# The function that executes the simulations
MC_easy <- function(dgp, estimator, seed, obs, reps) {
    # Set seed
    set.seed(seed)

    # Create the object to hold all the sim results
    MC_results <- NULL

    # Run the simulations
    for(i in 1:reps) {
        dat <- get(dgp)(obs)
        MC_results[[i]] <- get(estimator)(dat)
    }

    # Return the results
    return(do.call(rbind, MC_results))
}

# Define a function to draw one sample using the specified DGP
OLS_data <- function(nobs) {
    ## (Function contains the usual things you'd define for any MC simulation.) ##

    # Covariates
    z <- rnorm(nobs)
    x1 <- rnorm(nobs)
```

[11] http://www.econometricsbysimulation.com/2012/12/easy-monte-carlo-sampler-command.html

```
# Error draw
u <- rnorm(nobs)

# Generate true y
y <- 3 + 0.75*x1 + 3*z + 0.5*u  # TRUE DGP SPECIFIED HERE

# Return this 'sampled' dataset
return(data.frame(y, x1, z))
}

# Define a function to run the model of interest
OLS_est <- function(temp_data) {
  # Estimate the model
  lm <- lm(y ~ x1 + z, data=temp_data)

  # Grab the coefficients from the summary command.
  lm_coef <- coef(summary(lm))

  # Extract the column vector with all the coefficients
  lm_b <- c(lm_coef[,1])
  names(lm_b) <- paste0("b", 0:(length(lm_b)-1))

  # Extract the column vector with all the SEs
  lm_se <- c(lm_coef[,2])
  names(lm_se) <- paste0("se", 0:(length(lm_se)-1))

  # Return b and SE as single row vector
  return(c(lm_b, lm_se))
}

# Run the simulations. Do 500 draws, with each draw's dataset having 10 observations
res <- MC_easy(dgp="OLS_data," estimator="OLS_est," seed=838, obs=10, reps=500)
```
———————————————————— **Smart's original code (simplified)** ————————————————————

Smart's basic structure stays intact when we convert the code into a Shiny app. Figure 2.2 lays out the basic flow of `server.R` using whySurv, using the object and function names from the app's "Right Censoring" page.[12]

There are four major modifications we have to make for the Shiny conversion. All of these modifications occur in (what will become) `server.R`:

1. Having users click a button to start the simulations, to cut down on server load (Fig. 2.2's "START"). Otherwise, Shiny's reactivity[13] means it will start running a new batch of simulations *every* time the user changes a slider's value. The function triggered by the button press will return MC_easy()'s simulation results (Fig. 2.2's data_reg_cens()).

---

[12] The quotes in Fig. 2.2's "(Occurs 'First')" label allude to the label's stylized depiction of the app's execution order. The actual execution order is more complex (fn. 22), but the details are not crucial for making basic modifications or additions.

[13] https://shiny.rstudio.com/articles/reactivity-overview.html

2. For the simulation characteristics the user can adjust, inserting references to the corresponding widget values at the appropriate locations in `server.R` using `input$`*widgetNameHere* (assuming the widgets have been created in `ui.R`, which I discuss more in the next subsection).

3. Crafting a wrapper function to use as `MC_easy()`'s `estimator` argument. The function calls many individual estimator functions and then organizes the same dataset within a models using the same dataset within a draw (Fig. 2.2's `sim_est_cens()`).

4. Creating tables and/or graphs to display the simulation results using `server.R`'s `render*()` function(s) (and then, in `ui.R`, adding the corresponding `*output()` function).

Much of the above involves writing (what are technically) new functions in `server.R`. If the app is particularly complex, you can place these functions in separate R files to help with organization. `olsApp` does this, as does `whySurv` and `linRegEstms`. If you do the same, be sure to `source()` each separate R file inside of `server.R`'s `function(input,output,session)` segment. Also, be sure to specify `local=TRUE` as an option, to ensure the functions get sourced to the appropriate R environment.

What does all of this imply for editing the simulation apps? Continuing to use Figure 2.2's function names for concreteness, what you need to edit depends on what functionality you wish to add:

- **Modifying existing DGP**
  - Find the DGP's corresponding generation function (for the DGP responsible for generating right-censored data, Fig. 2.2's `cens_OLS _data()`
  - Make any desired modifications. Doing so will likely involve regular R skills more than Shiny-specific skills.
  - Once complete, ensure the returned object is still of the type expected by the app's other functions (if relevant).
- **New DGP**
  - Each DGP needs a corresponding function that generates one sampled dataset. The DGP function must return a data frame.
  - Add an `MC_easy()` call for every DGP you add, passing the name of the new DGP function to `MC_easy()`'s `dgp` argument. You could do this in one of two ways:
    1. Insert an additional call to `MC_easy()` from `data_reg_cens()`.
    2. Define a new function, also triggered by a button press, that calls `MC_easy()` (e.g., a function named `data_reg_nnorm()` for `whySurv`'s "Non-Normal Errors" page). All of Section 4's simulation apps use this second strategy because each page in these

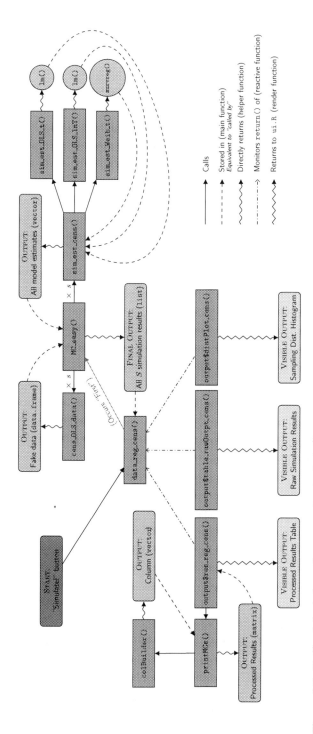

Figure 2.2 Stylized depiction of server.R, whySurv app.

apps represents a different DGP. Each page has its own unique

[Simulate!] button, which we can use to trigger the page's corresponding data...() function.

- Ensure the new simulation results get added to the object returned by data_reg_cens() (or the new data...() function, if you go that route).[14]
- Create any new outputs to display the results to the user. If you've modified the structure of data_reg_cens()'s returned object, verify the existing outputs still work as they should.

- **Modify existing model**
  - Find the model's corresponding model function (e.g., sim_est_OLS_t(), for estimating a linear model with untransformed y as the dependent variable)
  - Make any desired modifications. Doing so will likely involve regular R skills more than Shiny-specific skills.
  - Once complete, ensure the returned object is still of the type expected by the app's other functions (if relevant).

- **New model**
  - Define a new model function. At minimum, the model function must return a row vector with estimated coefficients and standard errors.
  - Add a call to the new model function from the model wrapper function, sim_est_cens().
  - Ensure the new simulation results get added to the object returned by sim_est_cens().
  - (You do not need to modify anything in MC_easy() because its estimator argument is already the model wrapper function, sim_est_cens().)
  - The last two bullets under "New DGP" now apply.

- **Modifying existing output**
  - "Main" tab, processed results table: output$res_reg_cens() renders the table via tableOutput(). printMCs processes the simulation output, binding together each of the table's columns, which are constructed using the colBuilder helper function. You will need to edit at least one of these two helper functions if you want to alter the table's contents.
    - Adjust number of rows: colBuilder
    - Adjust number of columns: printMCs

---

[14] If you opted to modify data_reg_cens(), notice how the function now acts as a wrapper for multiple DGP calls, similar to how sim_est_cens() acts as a wrapper for multiple model calls.

- "Raw Simulation Output" tab: `output$table_rawOutpt_cens()` calls the DT package's `dataTableOutput()` to produce the styled table.
- "Distribution Plot" tab: `output$distPlot_cens()` contains the `renderPlot()` call that generates the sampling distribution histograms. `whySurv` uses base R for its graphs, but `ggplot2` also works (e.g., see `olsApp`).

- **New visible output** (e.g., graph/table from simulations)
  - USING INFO ALREADY IN `data_reg_cens()`
    - Create new `render*()` function
    - Extract and manipulate the existing information to complete the `render*()` call
    - Insert the corresponding `*Output()` function in `ui.R`. Where you insert it will dictate where it appears visually.
  - USING INFO NOT ALREADY IN `data_reg_cens()`
    What this entails would depend on what additional information you require and where that information is coming from.
    As an example, `olsApp` has all the same features as `whySurv`, but also has additional tabs featuring simulation draw-specific graphs that require either the draw's *actual* `lm()` object and/or the draw's sampled dataset. If we wanted something similar in `whySurv`, it is currently impossible. `data_reg_cens()` returns neither the model objects nor the datasets, so they would need to be added:
    - Begin in `sim_est_cens()` because (1) the model results originate from here and (2) the draw's sampled dataset is also accessible from this function, allowing us to hit two birds with one stone. Currently, `sim_est_cens()` returns a row vector with the coefficients and standard errors. Change the returned object type to a list. The list's first element will be the row vector containing the model estimates (what the function currently returns). The list's second element can be the model object(s), which we can pass as (another) list (`whySurv` estimates multiple models for a single draw, hence the list). The returned object's third and final element is the sampled dataset for that draw, as a data frame.
    - Move up the chain to `MC_easy()`. If the function does not already aggregate its returned output as a list, make it so, such that the *i*th list item contains `sim_est_cens()`'s three-element list from the *i*th simulation draw. Return this new mega-list as `MC_easy()`'s output.
    - Move up the chain once again to `data_est_cens()`. Modify its returned object as needed such that it is also a list. Most likely, `data_est_cens()`'s returned object will be the same as `MC_easy()` with no modifications.

- Modify any of your existing `render*()`s (last bullet of "New DGP"). `data_est_cens()` still contains the same information as before, but organized differently. Extract the requisite info from `data_est_cens()`'s list and integrate it into the existing code. You may need to get creative with `unlist()`, `do.call()`, and/or `*apply()` when you extract, depending on how you structured the returned list object.
- The three bullets under "USING INFO ALREADY IN `data_reg_cens()`" now apply.

- **Modifying existing MathJax equation**
  - Find corresponding function in either `server.R` or `ui.R`. The function's location depends on whether the equation's contents are static or dynamic:
    - STATIC: Equations whose contents *do not update* based on any widget values are defined in `ui.R`.
    - DYNAMIC: Equations whose contents *do update* based on a widget's value are defined in `server.R`.
  - Make any desired modifications to MathJax code. If needed, use `paste()` to build the string of MathJax characters, as described below.
- **New MathJax equation**
  - Assuming the new equation involves dynamic information from the user (however indirectly), create a new output function with `renderUI()`.[15]
  - Extract any relevant information from the appropriate source, given your expression of interest.
    - If the equation involves any *output from the simulations*, extract and manipulate the relevant information from `data_reg_cens()` into the form you need.
    - If referring to *widget values*, you can refer to them directly using `input$widgetNameHere`.
  - Use `paste()` to build the string of MathJax characters, inserting the dynamic information where desired in the string.
  - Wrap the string in `withMathJax()` and make the wrapped string `renderUI()`'s returned object.
  - In `ui.R`, insert a `uiOutput()` call to your new `renderUI()` function where you want the new equation to appear.

---

[15] If there is no dynamic information, you can type the equation as static text in `ui.R`.

2.1.2 ui.R

ui.R contains all the information shiny needs to display your app to the user as a website: instructions about layout, which widgets to display and where, where to display the app's output, and both the presence and placement of any other static information like text, equations, or images.

ui.R's code automatically generates the HTML (Hypertext Markup Language) required for the app to be viewable as a website. Like all HTML, the app's appearance can be styled with CSS (Cascading Style Sheets). All six of the Element's apps, as well as whySurv, have at least one separate CSS file that ui.R loads using includeCSS() when the app launches. The main CSS file's name is style.css. All the aesthetic details not covered by shinythemes::shinytheme() are very likely defined in style.css; check there first if you are looking to tweak spacing, colors, fonts, and other features. You can also load the app in a browser and use the browser's built-in web inspector to pinpoint the CSS rule(s) you wish to tweak.

Overall Page Structure A single app can have many pages (Fig. 2.1's uppermost navigation bar, "Why Duration Models?"). In the simulation apps, each page represents a different violation of interest. We create each page (and its corresponding menu item) using tabPanel(), with each call creating a single page. (We eventually create the page's content by passing it along as arguments to tabPanel().) We pass these tabPanel() calls as arguments to navbarPage() to create the menu. whySurv has two pages; olsApp and linRegEstms, twelve.

To add a new page to any of the simulation apps, then, simply add an additional tabPanel() to navbarPage()'s argument list. The argument list's order dictates the order in which pages are listed in the menu.

Once a user selects a page, the simulation apps are further subdivided into one or more subpages. Users navigate between these subpages using navigation tabs (Fig. 2.1's "Main," "Raw Simulation Output," "Distribution Graph" tabs), with each tab representing a subpage. Similar to creating the larger pages, we create subpages with calls to tabPanel(), but we then pass these calls as arguments to tabsetPanel(), not navbarPage(). Adding a subpage is thus as easy as passing an additional tabPanel() to tabsetPanel(). Like before, the order in which we pass the arguments dictates the tabs' displayed order.

Organizationally, an app with many pages (and subpages) can be divided across R files, to help make the code more readable, just as we can split up server.R's functions across R files. olsApp, linRegEstms, and whySurv all use this strategy. For these apps, ui.R creates the app's navigation bar and overall page structure, but each individual page is contained in another R file loaded by ui.R. In these instances, editing a specific page or subpage is a matter of finding its corresponding individual R file within the app's directory.

To use the skeleton of whySurv's ui.R as an example:

```
————————————————————————  whySurv: ui.R  ————————————————————————
fluidPage(
    navbarPage("Why Duration Models?",
        # "Non-Normal Errors" page
        tabPanel("Non-Normal Errors",
            source("uiPt_nnorm.R", local=TRUE)$value
        ),
        # "Right Censoring" page
        tabPanel("Right Censoring",
            source("uiPt_cens.R", local=TRUE)$value
        )
    )
)
————————————————————————  whySurv: ui.R  ————————————————————————
```

ui.R contains the navbarPage() call necessary to create the app's overall structure, but each page's tabPanel() has source() as an argument.[16] The R file being sourced contains the page's content. That content includes the page's actual content (text, images, tables, graphs), as well as laying out the page's subpage structure (if present) and the content of those subpages.

To continue the example, consider the skeleton of uiPt_cens.R, which defines whySurv's "Right Censoring" page:

```
————————————————————————  whySurv: uiPt_cens.R  ————————————————————————
# File start
tabsetPanel(
    tabPanel("Main",
        # ... # app continues [code truncated]
    ),
    tabPanel("Raw Simulation Output",
        # ... # app continues [code truncated]
    ),
    tabPanel("Distribution Graph",
        # ... # app continues [code truncated]
    )
)
# File end
————————————————————————  whySurv: uiPt_cens.R  ————————————————————————
```

The "Right Censoring" page's R file opens with tabsetPanel(), which tells Shiny the page is composed of multiple subpages. This page has no content that displays across all subpages (other than the navigation and tab menu), evident

---

[16] source()$value prevents R from outputting a stray character to the app's UI.

in the absence of any code between the file's start and `tabsetPanel()`. Each subpage is subsequently defined with a `tabPanel()` call.[17] In the simulation apps, these subpages contain the actual content the user sees.

Individual Page Layout For all of Section 4's apps, the "Main" tab contains all the simulation settings. The information inputted by the user on this tab is required for the simulation apps to run (vs. the other tabs, which merely provide the user with additional post-estimation information).

All the simulation apps' "Main" tabs have the same layout: a sidebar on the left and a main content area on the right. This layout is invoked by calling `sidebarLayout()` with its default options and passing along two arguments: (1) `sidebarPanel()` and (2) `mainPanel()`:

1. **Left Sidebar**: The sidebar's contents are defined as arguments to `sidebarPanel()`. The order in which the arguments are passed dictates the order in which the corresponding content will appear in the sidebar.

   - The sidebar contains all of the simulation settings that the user can manipulate. Each setting has its own input widget, of which there are many basic[18] and extended[19] types. The widget type you choose depends on what information you want to gather from the user. If several widget types would work, `shiny` will not care which widget you pick—the choice is yours.

   - The sidebar also contains various clickable buttons. Each button's existence and appearance is defined in `ui.R`, but the actions triggered by clicking the button are defined in `server.R`.

     - All the simulation apps have a <kbd>🚀 Simulate!</kbd> button that begins a given simulation run.

     - Some of the simulation apps have additional buttons that appear in the sidebar as well, such as <kbd>🔀 Shuffle</kbd> (randomly pick parameter values), <kbd>🔄 Reset</kbd> (return all sliders to default values), and <kbd>📋 No Violation Scenario</kbd> (copying over the parameter values from the "No Violations" page, for expedience).

---

[17] If the subpages were particularly complex, if we wanted, we could employ the same `source()` trick for the subpages as we did in `ui.R` for the pages. `linRegEstms`'s pages do a variant of this for three of their four subpages; see `uiPt__tabBuildFuncts.R` if you wish to edit these subpages' content. The file also defines the contents of the main panel for `linRegEstms`' "Main" tabs.

[18] https://shiny.rstudio.com/gallery/widget-gallery.html

[19] http://shinyapps.dreamrs.fr/shinyWidgets/

2. **Main Panel**: The panel's contents are defined as arguments to mainPanel().
   Like the sidebar, the order in which the arguments are passed to
   mainPanel() dictates the order in which the corresponding content will
   appear in the panel.

   - The panel contains the processed results table for the simulations, at min-
     imum. The table's contents are defined in server.R. Look to that file if
     you want to add (or subtract) rows or columns from the results table, as I
     mentioned earlier (p. 16).
   - Very often, the simulation app will also have LATEX equations, rendered
     with MathJax, that appear above the processed results table. I discussed
     editing these equations earlier (p. 18).

To wrap up, when it comes to making ui.R modifications:

- If you intend to **add components to the simulation**, like another parameter input for users to set, you will need to modify the "Main" tab by
  adding widgets corresponding to the new components. (At present, all the
  simulation-related widgets appear in the left sidebar.) You will also need to
  insert the new widget's value into the appropriate location(s) in server.R
  (discussed in Sect. 2.1.1).
- If you want to **add additional output** from the current simulations, like
  another graph, we could add it to the "Main" tab's main panel. However,
  you will likely want to add a new subpage instead. Nothing about shiny's
  syntax necessitates as much, but for organizational purposes, doing so helps
  break the output into manageable chunks for your user.

2.1.3 global.R

global.R is an optional file, but nearly all of the Element's apps use it.
global.R is automatically executed when a Shiny app runs. It is useful because
its contents can be called by either server.R or ui.R. The Element apps'
library() statements usually appear in global.R. For some of the apps,
global.R also has smaller R files that it source()s, containing common
functions, lists, or text that need to be defined once, but also need to be glob-
ally sourced because they are referenced in several of the app's R files (e.g.,
ui.R/server.R, multiple UI pages).

2.2 Estimation Method Apps (leastSq, mleLM, leastSqLASSO)

The other app cluster pertains to estimation methods. These apps are easier
to modify because they have fewer moving pieces, despite first appearances

Table 2.2 Estimation Method Apps, Quick Reference
Table

Modification	New/Existing
Adapting to new model (`server.R, ui.R`)	p. 26
Saving DGP's true parameter values (`server.R`)	p. 27
Setting prose style to "Formal," permanently (`ui.R`)	p. 28

(see Table 2.2 for quick reference). I use `leastSq` as the running example because it is the simpler of Section 3's apps.

2.2.1 server.R

Figure 2.3 depicts the stylized layout of `leastSq`'s `server.R`.[20] The diagram looks more complex than Figure 2.2, but only because (1) the estimation method apps need to continually react to the sliders, so they have many more reactive functions,[21] and (2) `leastSq` needs far more outputs to achieve its purpose. Accordingly, I do not simplify the majority of the outputs away in what follows.

Descriptively, the app's `server.R` works in this way:

1. Users select their n and random seed, then click ⊞ Generate Fake Data (Fig. 2.3's blue START box at upper left).
2. The button click triggers a series of functions (Fig. 2.3's top half). Nothing the user does from this point affects the information these functions use. As a result, they only need to execute once.
   - `dataGen()` draws a random true value for α and for β, then uses these values to generate a single fake dataset using the model's corresponding DGP.
   - `all()` takes `dataGen()`'s dataset and finds the actual least-squares estimates. The data, actual estimates, and smallest $\sum \hat{u}^2$ get returned by `all()` for other functions to reference.

---

[20] See fn. 12 regarding the quotes in the figure's "(Occurs 'First')".

[21] By contrast, the simulation apps only react when users press .

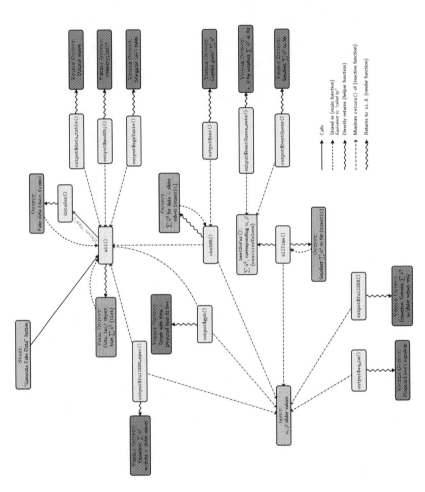

Figure 2.3 Stylized depiction of server.R, leastSq app.

- The dataset is immediately available for users to view (output$data
  _table(); first in the trio of output$/VISIBLE OUTPUT boxes at Fig. 2.3's
  upper right). Once the user clicks ⚠ Show Answer , the app also displays the actual results to the user in two formats (bottom two outputs in
  upper-right trio).

3. The user begins interacting with the α and β sliders in a quest to find the
   line minimizing the sum of squares (Fig. 2.3's bottom half). There are many
   reactive functions – functions that "listen" to the sliders and automatically
   re-execute when any of the sliders' values change (dash-dotted arrows with
   simple arrow heads in Fig. 2.3).[22] Three major actions occur every time α's
   or β's slider value changes:

- **Graph**
  - The app takes all()'s returned dataset, plots it, and superimposes
    the proposed line corresponding to the user's selected slider values
    (output$gph()).
  - The app also prints out the proposed line's equation (output$eq_lm()).
- **Sum-of-squares equations**
  - The app calculates the sum of squared residuals for all()'s returned
    dataset and the user's proposed line (obsSSR()) and displays the
    information to the user (output$ssr()).
  - The app builds the LaTeX code to display (what amounts to)
    obsSSR()'s step-by-step calculations. It outputs the $\sum \hat{u}^2$ expression
    with y and x expressed generically, but with the specific slider values
    inserted for α and β (output$fullSSR()). It then inserts the dataset's
    specific x and y values and prints the entire $\sum \hat{u}^2$ expression term by
    term (output$fullSSR_spec()). Both of these equations are printed
    to the ◉ pop-up box in "Formal" prose mode.
- **Keeping track of best guess**
  - The app compares obsSSR()'s $\sum \hat{u}^2$ with the lowest $\sum \hat{u}^2$ value found
    by the user in this app session (allTime() does the comparing).
    This all-time low is stored as ssr in the bestSoFar reactive values
    object.[23] Additionally, bestSoFar$ssr's value is always displayed to

---

[22] For more on reactivity, see RStudio's overview at https://shiny.rstudio.com/articles/
understanding-reactivity.html. The key is conceiving of reactive functions as proverbial black
holes that immediately and indiscriminately *pull* the information they need from the functions
whose output they monitor when that output changes, rather than those monitored functions
pushing the information downstream to the reactive functions, like a torrent of water.

[23] You can conceive of a reactive value object as having global scope within server.R, but that
globalness only extends to a specific app session (vs. all sessions of the app running at that time
on the server, which would be the case if we used a conventional R global object).

the user (output$bestGuess(), last in trio of VISIBLE OUTPUT boxes at Fig. 2.3's lower right).

- If bestSoFar$ssr $<$ obsSSR()'s $\sum \hat{u}^2$, the app does nothing.
- If bestSoFar$ssr $\geq$ obsSSR()'s $\sum \hat{u}^2$, obsSSR()'s value gets stored as the new best in bestSoFar$ssr. The α and β values corresponding to this guess are also stored in bestSoFar (with element names alG and b1G, respectively). These values are also displayed to the user, after clicking ⚠ Show Answer (output$bestGuess_ests()).

4. When the user clicks ⚠ Show Answer , in addition to the output already noted above, the app also outputs the actual $\sum \hat{u}^2$ (output function omitted from Fig. 2.3 for simplicity) and the actual $\{\alpha, \beta\}$ least-squares values (function also omitted) from all().

The most expansive potential modification for the estimation method apps is to implement the app for an entirely different estimator. We would need to make changes associated with each of the three actions above, as well as changes in the app's behavior before the data are even generated. Certain code changes are necessary for some models, but not others. I use mleLM and mleLogit, the ML apps for a linear and logit model, respectively, as concrete examples to illustrate the changes to leastSq. The parentheses at the end of each bullet note whether changes are or are not involved for the corresponding app.

- **Pre-Data Generation**
  - Add sliders to the "Main" tab's sidebar for each additional parameter involved with the estimation method beyond α and β (yes for mleLM [σ_u], no for mleLogit)
  - For each additional new parameter in dataGen(), add a line to randomly pick the new parameter's true value (yes for mleLM, no for mleLogit)
  - Initialize one new element inside bestSoFar for each additional new parameter (yes for mleLM, no for mleLogit)
  - Change dataGen()'s DGP to match that assumed by the estimator (no for mleLM, yes for mleLogit)
- **Graph**
  - Change the quantity appearing on the main graph's vertical axis (no for mleLM, yes for mleLogit)
  - Change the plotted line's functional form to match the estimator's assumed DGP (no for mleLM, yes for mleLogit)

- Add an additional graph, if needed, to illustrate the role of any auxiliary parameters in the estimation process (yes for `mleLM`, no for `mleLogit`)
- Modify the LATEX equation displaying the proposed line's equation (yes for `mleLM` [adding σ_u], yes for `mleLogit`)

- **Objective Functions (sum-of-squares/likelihood equations)**
  - Change `obsSSR()`'s calculation for the objective function to match the estimator's DGP (yes for both)
  - Modify `output$fullSSR()`'s LATEX equation for the generic objective function's output (yes for both)
  - Modify `output$fullSSR_spec()`'s LATEX equation for the specific objective function. The R function builds the objective function's full expression by iterating over each observation in the dataset and forming the term it contributes to $\sum \hat{u}^2$ or $\ln L$ (yes for both)

- **Keeping track of best guess**
  - Flip `allTime()`'s inequalities if looking for maximum likelihood (vs. minimum sum of squares) (yes for both)
  - For each new parameter, add a line in `allTime()` to store that parameter's value for the user's best guess so far into `bestSoFar` (yes for `mleLM`, no for `mleLogit`)

Another, smaller desirable modification may be storing the true values of α and β. At present, the two parameters' true values are sampled within `dataGen()`, but are stored no further. If we wanted access to these values elsewhere, we would need to (1) shift `dataGen()` to return a list and have the two true parameter values be elements of that returned list (see p. 17, USING INFO NOT ALREADY IN DATA–REG–CENS() header for an example), followed by (2) having `all()` return the two true parameter values as part of its returned list. The values will then be accessible to the app's other functions.

2.2.2 `ui.R`

The same general points from Section 2.1.2 apply here. In the terminology of that section, each estimation method app comprises a single page with two subpages. The "Main" tab has the same sidebar–main panel layout as the simulation apps' "Main" tabs. The "Data" tab has the same layout as the simulation apps' "Raw Simulation Output" tabs.

Unlike the simulation app `ui.R`s, the estimation method app `ui.R`s use many more `conditionalPanel()`s – UI functions that reveal their contents only when certain conditions are met. Any website can have conditionally hidden information using JavaScript, another web-based programming language. `conditionalPanel()` is a convenience wrapper from `shiny` that

spares us from writing the relevant raw JavaScript code. The apps use the
`conditionalPanel()`s to ensure (a) no information shows in `leastSq`'s
main panel until a dataset exists, as well as (b) the true least-squares estimates are revealed only after the user clicks [⚠ Show Answer] (Fig. 2.3's
`output$bestGuess_ests()`). The conditions of note are (given in the syntax
that `conditionalPanel()`'s `condition` argument expects):

- `input.dataGenButton!=0`: `dataGenButton` returns a count of how many
  times the button has been clicked. Panels with this `condition` argument,
  then, are to remain hidden until the user generates a fake dataset.
- `input.solnButton==0` (or `!=0`): same idea as above, only for
  [⚠ Show Answer]. A value of 0 means the button hasn't been clicked; the
  user is still trying to find the smallest sum of squares using the sliders, and
  therefore, the `conditionalPanel()`'s contents should stay hidden. By contrast, a nonzero value means the user has requested the solution be displayed;
  the `conditionalPanel()`'s contents should be shown.

The language changes between "Informal"/"Formal" prose are also imple-
mented using the same JavaScript functionality, but using the `shinyjs`
package's `hide()` and `show()` convenience functions. The text's initial con-
dition is defined in `ui.R` (e.g., `hidden("text that will be hidden to
start here")`), but *when* to subsequently show or hide the text is defined in
`server.R`. `input$lang` corresponds to the upper-right switch that controls
which text should be shown, with a value of `TRUE` corresponding to informal
language and `FALSE` corresponding to formal language.

If you want to get rid of the informal/formal language distinction, the easiest
way to do it is to (1) set the switch's value to the logical value associated with
the prose style you always want displayed, and (2) hide the switch from users
using JavaScript, rather than deleting it entirely. Hiding the switch permits its
value to still be accessible to the app's other parts, saving you from having to
root out all the `shinyjs` conditional code about which content to display when.

If, for instance, you wanted the *formalized* language always displayed, you
would need to switch the following line of code

―――――――――――――――― `ui.R` switch snippet, original ――――――――――――
```
switchInput("lang", "Prose Style", value = TRUE,
            onLabel="Informal", offLabel="Formal",
            size="small", inline=TRUE)
```
―――――――――――――――― `ui.R` switch snippet, original ――――――――――――

to read

```
————————————— ui.R switch snippet, modified ————————————
hidden(                                              # NEW
    switchInput("lang", "Prose Style", value = FALSE,   # MODIFIED (value arg)
                onLabel="Informal", offLabel="Formal",
                size="small", inline=TRUE)
)                                                    # NEW
————————————— ui.R switch snippet, modified ————————————
```

3 Defining "Best": Estimation

Section 3 is the first of three sections focusing on the Element's actual apps. Its focus is the two major ways in which we can define a line as "best fitting" a set of data: least squares and maximum likelihood.

3.1 Section's App Overview

3.1.1 Descriptions

This section's activities involve two apps:

- leastSq (Sect. 3.3) [https://bit.ly/347SCeL]: Focuses on the intuition behind the least-squares line. Students manually minimize the sum of squares for a randomly generated set of data by selecting various slope and intercept values. The app displays a graph with the proposed best-fit line superimposed over the fake data. The line updates based on students' slope + intercept selections.
- mleLM (Sect. 3.4) [https://bit.ly/39fDWe1]: Focuses on the intuition behind maximum likelihood. Students manually find the maximum of a linear model's likelihood function for a randomly generated set of data. Like leastSq, mleLM displays a graph with the proposed best-fit line and fake data, and this line updates as students select different slope + intercept values.[24]

leastSqLASSO also falls under this header, as it finds the best-fit line for a LASSO model. It appears in Section 5, with the other LASSO app, for thematic reasons.

3.1.2 Major Points

You can use these apps to demonstrate the following points. The list is not exhaustive. For a more detailed discussion of a given app's features, refer to the relevant subsection noted above. Section 3.5 gives a series of example activities focused on developing students' intuition about the two estimation methods.

---

[24] I also have several variants of this app complete for nonlinear models (e.g., logit, multinomial logit), available elsewhere (https://github.com/MetzgerSK/shinyAdvReg).

- From basic geometry, we know $A = a^2$ represents the area of a square with dimensions $a \times a$. To speak of $\hat{u}^2$, then, means we have a square with dimensions $\hat{u} \times \hat{u}$...

  ❯ `leastSq`, generate set of fake data. Move sliders to illustrate how the shaded squares, representing $\hat{u}_i^2$, change in size depending on our guesses for α and β.

- ...and "minimizing the sum of squared residuals" thus means making the collective area of all the shaded squares as small as possible.

  ❯ `leastSq`, generate set of fake data, move sliders to try to find smallest sum of squares.

- The sum of squared residuals is not displayed in R's `summary(lm())` output. However, we can calculate it from the available information.

  ❯ `leastSq`, generate set of data, click **⚠ Show Answer**. Scroll to bottom of "Main" tab and select "R Output" subtab. $\sum \hat{u}^2 = $ `Residual standard error`^{2} $*$ `(residual) degrees of freedom`.

- Maximum likelihood deals with hypotheticals. It asks "if the true relationship between y and x is represented by this line I've guessed, how likely is it I'd see the actual y and x values I have in my dataset?"

  ❯ `mleLM`, generate set of fake data. (A smaller n makes this point less tedious to show.) Fiddle with sliders to illustrate general idea. Then, click the upper-right switch for "Formal" prose, followed by 👁 . Consider how the likelihood is formulated: it uses what we know about (1) probability density functions and (2) joint probabilities of independent events to express the "likeliness" of seeing our specific dataset's values, if the slope, intercept, and σ_u were equal to the values we're proposing.

- The error's variance, σ_u^2, is indirectly estimated in least squares. By contrast, the estimate is explicitly included when estimating a linear model with maximum likelihood.

  ❯ `leastSq`, generate set of fake data. There is no σ_u slider,[25] and σ_u never appears in the sum of squares calculations (select "Formal" prose using upper-right switch, then 👁). Now, open `mleLM`, generate set of fake data. σ_u now has a slider, and it also features prominently in the likelihood calculations (visible via "Formal," then 👁 , as before).

- MLE's properties are asymptotic. In smaller samples, its estimates of σ_u will be biased downward as a byproduct of its σ_u formula using n instead of $n - k - 1$ in the denominator ($k = $ number of regressors).

---

[25] Given variance of σ_u^2, standard deviation $= \sigma_u$.

> See Exercise 3.3, Q4'sinstructions, except set $n = 6$. The DGPs are identical, so `mleLM`'s and `leastSq`'s point estimates will match, but `mleLM`'s σ_u and standard errors will be smaller than they should be, given the amount of uncertainty in the data, evident when you contrast them with `leastSq`'s output.

- When all the classic linear regression assumptions are met, $y \sim \mathcal{N}(XB, \sigma_u)$. This implies it's possible to find the ML best-fit line using only a histogram of the residuals from our current guesses of $\{\alpha, \beta, \sigma_u\}$, overlaid with a normal distribution.

  > `mleLM`, generate set of fake data. Focus only on the "Main" tab's right-hand graph. Changing the intercept and slope sliders will shift the histogram bars to the left or right. Eyeballing the graph, make the histogram's apparent mean match the overlaid normal distribution's mean. Next, match the overlaid normal's dispersion to the histogram's dispersion. Click **⚠ Show Answer**, compare the log-likelihood's true value to your all-time best guess.

- Each observation contributes a term to the model's log-likelihood. That term's formula derives from the assumptions we make about the error term's distribution...

  > `mleLM`, generate set of fake data. (A smaller n makes this point less tedious to show.) Fiddle with the sliders if desired. Go to the "Data" tab, look at the last column ("logLH_i"). It contains each observation's contribution to the log-likelihood. The generic formula, as well as the formula with specific values inserted, is viewable by clicking the upper-right switch for "Formal" prose on the "Main" tab, then **◉**. (See also Exercise 3.4.)

  (> For $\sum \hat{u}^2$ instead of ln$L$: `leastSq`, same steps as above. The "Data" tab's last column is named "uHatSq.")

- ...and the model log-likelihood's involves summing across all these individual contributions.

  > Same as previous point's first bullet, but click **⚠ Show Answer**. Go to the "Data," manually add together all the "logLH_i" values on the "Data" tab. The total will match the value at the table's bottom, as well as the value under "Actual answer" on the "Main" tab.[26]

  (> For $\sum \hat{u}^2$: Same as this point's first bullet, only for previous point's second bullet.)

---

[26] There may be some small discrepancies across the two tabs' values because of rounding error from the sliders.

3.2 Introductory Remarks

3.2.1 Generalities

"How does the computer 'know' which regression line fits best?" is a question about *estimation*. The two most common estimation methods are least squares, usually discussed in the context of OLS, and maximum likelihood estimation (MLE), usually discussed in the context of generalized linear models. Students usually understand the two methods both pertain to regression. They might also understand that OLS can be estimated with MLE (because, with our imprecise way of speaking at times, we really mean "a classic linear model" when we say "OLS"). Understanding that the two estimation methods have more in common with one another than the word "regression," though, becomes more precarious. Students tend to see the separate models using each method as distinct silos, likely as a by-product of how we must divide up the material into different courses. The precariousness should be troublesome to instructors, because the two methods share a clear common thread, one that – were students more aware of it – would permit them to consolidate their knowledge about estimation methods, raising the chances they could recall it (and correctly) in new, future contexts.

Aside from the content usually being featured in different courses, one potential contributing factor to the precariousness is the static way in which we discuss these estimation methods:

- For least squares, we often motivate the discussion by graphing some toy data with the best-fit line superimposed, allowing us to then emphasize how the least-squares line will have the smallest distance between it and the data points (= the residual, $\hat{u}$). Students may also solve for the least-squares estimates for a toy dataset or two, and perhaps also derive the basic formulas for α and β using calculus and first-order conditions.
- For maximum likelihood, students get the algebraic expressions for a basic likelihood, along with a verbal explanation of the technique. At most (typically), students work out the ML estimate for a small toy example. They also perhaps have static graphs of a log-likelihood function and how we work step-by-step to find the log-likelihood's maximum.

The common theme for both is that students get various pieces of the puzzle – static graphs, equations, small toy datasets – but lack an accessible way to put them together easily to facilitate deeper understanding, both within each topic and across the topics.

Shiny's ability to show content *dynamically* provides a student-centric way to connect the pieces. The two methods' commonality is that both define a rule to determine which line is best fitting. They differ in what that rule is, giving rise to the two methods' different names (and, thus, two different Shiny apps). Each app prominently features its method's chosen best-fit rule to highlight the main difference between least squares and MLE using a graph. Students get hands-on experience finding a parameter's estimate by proposing guesses for α's and β_1's estimated values,[27] and seeing how the graph changes, given an app's definition of best fit. At the same time, the apps emphasize the methods' commonality by having a similar visual structure, allowing students to draw parallels between various pieces of information across the apps, purely by virtue of where the information appears. These parallels can be reinforced with unlimited worked examples of various sample sizes, since R can easily generate infinite random examples.

3.2.2 Own Class Usage Examples

Undergraduate, Basic Regression. I may informally give students leastSq's link at the end of the class before the OLS lecture. If I do, I mention the app may be worth experimenting with, especially if the assigned reading's more mathy bits trip them up, but I stop short of making the app an official pre-class exercise. The app shows up in earnest in the middle of the OLS lecture, after discussing various aspects of least squares' definition. Depending on time constraints, I either (a) go through the spirit of Exercise 3.1 aloud, asking students what various pieces of the graph represent, given what we just discussed, or (b) break them into pairs or triplets and task them with answering the same "in spirit of" questions for about 5 minutes before reconvening. If the students did not have access to the app's link previously, I include it in the slides for that day, for them to experiment with later, if desired.

The next lecture, I open with a small activity in which students are given four data points with three candidate lines drawn through them. The instructions state one of the lines is the OLS best-fit line. Students are then told to determine which of the lines is the OLS line *without* performing the actual regression. (To do so, they need to apply the sum-of-squares definition by hand.)

Graduate, Basic Regression. Either as a pre-class activity or in previous coursework (like the department's math pre-fresher), students complete some variant of Exercise 3.2; I tell them to look over this past work, if it was completed for another course. I also assign Exercise 3.1 as a pre-class activity,

---

[27] Given a data-generating process [DGP] of the form $y = g(\alpha + \beta x)$, with $g(\cdot)$ representing some link function.

adding a question about the link between the past work and `leastSq`. The lecture starts with the usual pre-class activities discussion (see p. 6), then proceeds similar to the undergrad OLS class, with the freed-up time from the longer mid-class app discussion going toward the additional material that needs to be covered with graduate students.

Graduate, GLM/MLE. My graduate-level methods classes meet twice a week for 75 minutes. The meeting frequency is irrelevant for the basic regression course, but relevant for dividing up the material in the GLM/MLE course. One lecture goes toward reviewing OLS, and a second goes toward laying out the basics of MLE.

For the first lecture (OLS review), students get Exercise 3.1 as a pre-class activity and are told to review their OLS notes. Lecture opens similarly to the grad basic regression lecture on the same topic, but then I do one of two things. For option A, I break students into smaller groups and task them with broadly sketching out how they would teach *me* OLS. I give them about 15–25 minutes, with the groups conferring with one another toward the end of the allotted time before we reconvene. We spend the rest of class talking through the various broad plans, using them to review. Alternatively, for option B, we start the first of the Monte Carlo simulation lectures, since understanding a model's assumed DGP is a major part of writing simulations, providing an opportunity for review while also covering some new ground.

The second lecture on MLE basics comes a few lectures after the OLS review, with how many lectures after depending on whether I went with option A or B for the earlier lecture. Students complete Exercise 3.4 either as a pre-class activity or in previous coursework (like the department's math pre-fresher); I tell them to look over this past work if it was completed for another course. I also assign Exercise 3.3 as a pre-class activity, adding a question about the link between the past work and `mleLM`. For lecture, we go through the usual for pre-class activities (see p. 6), then proceed through the lecture. I make use of `mleLM`'s ability to display the likelihood expression at various points during the discussion.

3.3 The App: `leastSq` [https://bit.ly/347SCeL]

The `leastSq` app illustrates the intuition behind OLS. It generates a small set of fake data using a single covariate,[28] plots it, and permits students to drag sliders to set the intercept and slope of a straight line through (or near) these data points.

---

[28] σ_u is fixed at 1.5 for `leastSq`. This will not be the case for `mleLM`.

3.3.1 "Main" Tab

The app's "Main" tab is displayed upon loading the app. Students begin by selecting their dataset size using the n slider and setting the random seed (if desired).[29] Double clicking the n slider enables larger dataset sizes; the slider also changes color to signal the ranges are not the app's default. Double clicking again returns the slider back to its default ranges (and color). This ability exists in five of the Element's six apps.[30] Clicking `Generate Fake Data` creates the dataset and unhides the α and β sliders, allowing students to begin interacting with them.

The "Main" tab also contains the graph that auto-displays the squared residuals for each data point, given the current proposed line. The resultant image is striking (Figure 3.1). It helps students to realize just what "squared residuals" (and then the sum of them) means, at an intuitive level – the computer is trying to find the line that makes the size of the figure's translucent squares as small as possible, if you were to add all of their areas together. The `What's going on here?` button links to a pop-up box that gives students a broad overview of what the app does, and the role they play in that process.

To encourage students to experiment, the app keeps track of the smallest sum of squares value they have found so far. Clicking `Restore` sets the sliders to the slope and intercept values corresponding to that best guess.

Once students have sufficiently experimented to find the smallest sum of squares, clicking `Show Answer` will reveal the actual smallest sum of squares (Figure 3.2). Underneath the figure, the app also prints the actual model results, for reference, both as a nicely formatted Stargazer table and as raw `summary()` output. The latter is useful for reinforcing to students where the app's various quantities appear in R's output.

In addition to the all the above, the app permits students to connect the figure's visual with the underlying least-squares math. By default, the app's wording deliberately avoids key terms, to prompt students to think through what they observe, rather than immediately falling back on technical language – and the language's corresponding mental shortcuts. Clicking the upper-right switch to "Formal" shifts the app into more formal language (e.g., "smallest point total" for informal, "smallest sum of squares" for formal). While in

---

[29] The random seed guarantees students will get the same values from the random number generator. If you want students to get different results from one another, tell them to change the seed.

[30] `LASSO_bchamp` is the exception because it has no n slider.

Least Squares: The Intuition

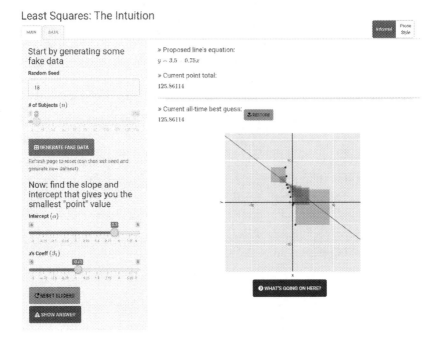

Figure 3.1 `leastSq`, "Main" tab.
Package version: `shiny_1.4.0.2`

"Formal" mode, a new 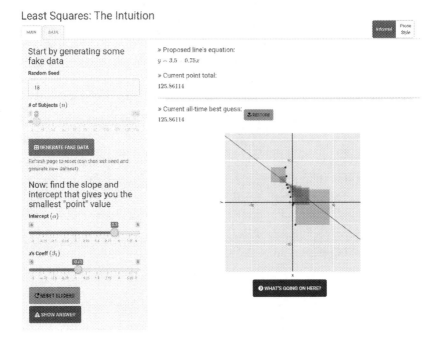 button becomes available for students to click, to the right of the main panel's "Current..." header. Doing so opens a movable pop-up window containing two sets of equations (Fig. 3.3). The first set is the generic expression for the sum of squared residuals with the student's selected slope and intercept values inserted. The second set is the same expression with the fake dataset's specific values inserted.

3.3.2 "Data" Tab

The "Data" tab displays the fake dataset whose values appear in the "Main" tab's graph (Fig. 3.4). Students can download a copy of the dataset locally by clicking [⬇ Download]. In the app, students can sort the data based on a variable's values and adjust how many observations they wish to view at a time (if $n > 25$, for the latter). The output also includes the $\hat{u}^2$ value for each observation as a third column, labeled "uHatSq."

3.4 The App: `mleLM` [https://bit.ly/39fDWe1]

We can write a similar Shiny app for maximum likelihood (ML), in which students search for the slope–intercept combination that maximizes the log-likelihood function for a set of data. The app's DGP has a continuous dependent

Least Squares: The Intuition

Figure 3.2 `leastSq`, Answer Revealed, "Main" tab.
Package version: `shiny_1.4.0.2`

variable and single covariate, same as `leastSq`. Similar to `leastSq`'s striking visual in Figure. 3.1, `mleLM`'s allows students to see what happens when someone tells the computer to estimate a regression with ML (Fig. 3.5): the computer goes out and looks for the combination of slope(s) and intercept values (and any other relevant parameter(s), given model type) that maximizes the regression's likelihood function.

Students perform the same general steps upon loading `mleLM` as they did for `leastSq`. Like before, they can double click the n slider to enable different dataset sizes than the default.[31] The functionality exists to provide comparable

---

[31] Large datasets are `mleLM`'s default; double clicking enables smaller datasets, in this case. Notably, the app does *not* warn students about MLE's properties only being guaranteed asymptotically.

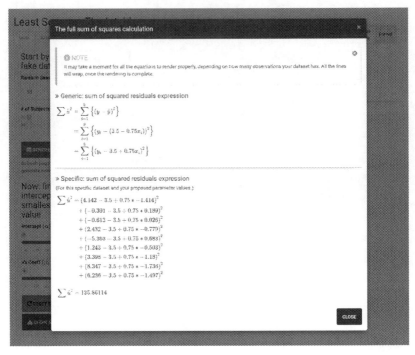

Figure 3.3 `leastSq`, Sum of Squares pop-up.
Package version: `shiny_1.4.0.2`

Least Squares: The Intuition

ID	y	x1	uHatSq
1	4.142	-1.414	0.176
2	-0.801	0.189	13.390
3	-0.613	0.026	16.756
4	2.432	-0.779	2.730
5	-5.363	0.883	69.725
6	1.243	-0.503	5.940
7	3.398	-1.180	0.975
8	8.347	-1.736	12.568
9	6.236	-1.497	2.602

TOTAL (across all 9 observations): 125.861

Figure 3.4 `leastSq`, "Data" tab.
Package version: `shiny_1.4.0.2`

sample sizes between `mleLM` and `leastSq`. To make the two apps use exactly the same data, students must match the *n*, seed, and click the "Make comparable with `leastSq`" checkbox in `mleLM`. Clicking 🔘, next to the checkbox, provides a reminder of which widgets' values need to match across the apps. The checkbox governs σ_u's true value. By default, `mleLM` randomly draws a σ_u value, because σ_u is an explicit part of the ML procedure (as I discuss more in a moment), making variation in its value across fake datasets desirable. Selecting the checkbox sets `mleLM`'s $\sigma_u = 1.5$, the same as it is in `leastSq`.

Otherwise, `mleLM` has the same features as `leastSq`, with one exception. A linear model's likelihood function for a bivariate DGP involves not only the slope and intercept, but also the error term's variance, σ_u^2. (σ_u is what ultimately appears in the app.) However, changing σ_u's proposed value brings about no visible change in the main x versus y graph, even though the displayed likelihood will change in value. To reinforce visually that something *is* occurring when σ_u changes, `mleLM`'s "Main" tab has a second graph that displays the residuals' distribution as a histogram + kernel plot, given the currently selected α and β values. The graph also has an overlaid normal distribution with mean 0 and standard deviation of σ_u. This second graph updates whenever σ_u's slider value changes, with the idea being the normal distribution's dispersion needs to match $\hat{u}$'s dispersion as closely as possible. Above the graphs, the numbered headers give students a heuristic suggestion as to which graph to focus on first. Clicking ❓ What's going on here? and scrolling to the pop-up window's bottom further acknowledges the heuristic.

The 👁 pop-up box also merits a further mention. While `mleLM` has the same general features as `leastSq`'s 👁, ML's underlying math is more complex than least squares', resulting in the pop-up having additional information. `mleLM` writes out the generic expressions for both the linear model's likelihood and its log-likelihood (Fig. 3.6). It then writes out the *entire* log-likelihood calculation specific to the generated dataset and the student's proposed parameter estimates, printing a term for every observation in the dataset. Everything is broadly the same as `leastSq`, up to this point. However, `mleLM` provides *two* versions of the dataset-specific log-likelihood expression, both of which are off screen in Fig. 3.6: (1) an unsimplified expression (e.g., products still being logged, exp() and ln() still present), which `leastSq` has no equivalent of, and (2) a simplified expression, just as `leastSq` does.[32]

Printing out the log-likelihood provides sizable pedagogical benefits, relative to comparable non-Shiny activities. We rarely write out the entire log-likelihood calculation when we teach in a regression context, mostly because

---

[32] The app includes $-0.5 \ln(2\pi)$ in its likelihood expressions so that its calculated $\ln L$ matches the hand-rolled $\ln L$ from `stats4::mle()`'s help file ($\geq$ R 4.0). Exercise 3.4's extension question (Q6) asks students about the term.

MLE: The Intuition - Linear Models

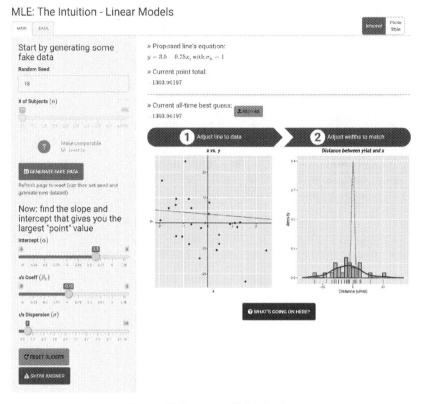

Figure 3.5 `mleLM`, "Main" tab.
Package version: `shiny_1.4.0.2`

of its tedium. If we do write it out, the typical example dataset is extremely small. But, with Shiny, writing the expression is automated, allowing you to display it very quickly for a dataset of any size. Further, there is no chance of a dropped sign, omitted natural log, misplaced parenthesis, or a mistyped α, β_1, or x value appearing in the printed expression, provided you have correctly written the code assembling the log-likelihood's MathJax expression in the first place. As a result, students get to see increasingly complex, fully written log-likelihood expressions that, otherwise, they would not, let alone expressions with dynamically updating components for infinitely many examples.

3.5 Example Activities

The following example activities stem from a situation in which the lecture's main intended learning outcomes involve students being able to (1) intuitively describe each estimation method, (2) explain how the methods are similar and different, (3) identify and apply basic ideas from a math pre-fresher in context,

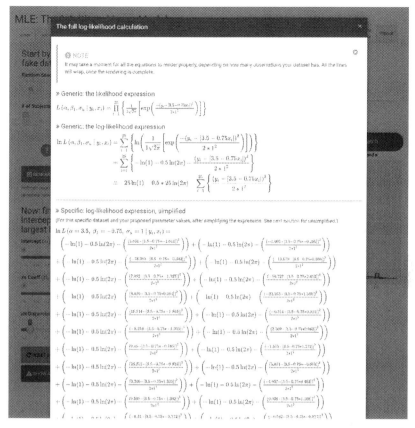

Figure 3.6 `mleLM`, Likelihood pop-up.
Package version: `shiny_1.4.0.2`

and (4) connect the intuition they describe to certain pieces of each method's underlying math.

Exercise 3.1: Least Squares: Linear Model (Pre-Class)

1. Load `leastSq` and experiment with the app. Informally, what does the app's focus seem to be?

2. How is an observation's squared residual depicted in the figure?

3. Visually, what does that imply the graph should look like if we were trying to *minimize* the squared residuals across all the observations?

Exercise 3.2: Least Squares: Linear Model (Longer)

1. Using `leastSq`, set seed to 101 and $n = 5$. Generate a fake dataset and try to find the line of best fit using the sliders. Make note of what your eventual α and β values are, once you seem to find the smallest sum of squares.

2. Consider the equation under "Proposed line's equation." Write out the expression for single observation's residual using Greek symbols for the unknown parameter values – what is it equal to?

3. Find the value of the squared residual for an observation.

4. Mathematically, how would we generically express the *sum* of the observations' squared residuals (hereafter, SSR)?

5. Using (4), find the partial derivative of the SSR with respect to α.

6. Set (5) equal to zero and solve for α.

7. Returning (4), find the partial derivative of the SSR with respect to β.

8. Set (7) equal to zero and solve for β.

9. Go to the app's "Data" tab. Plug the data's y and x values into your expressions from (6) and (8). Simplify the expressions.

10. Click [⚠ Show Answer], compare the actual answers to your answers from (9). With this comparison in mind, explain the rationale behind each of the steps we took in (4)–(9). *(If needed explicitly: Why does taking these steps result in our hand-calculated estimates having the same value as the actual model estimates?)*

Exercise 3.3: MLE: Linear Model (Pre-Class)

1. Load `mleLM` and experiment with the app. Informally, what does the app's focus seem to be?

2. What is the key concept underlying maximum likelihood? Where is it evident in the app?

3. What is `leastSq`'s key concept? Describe one similarity and one difference between (2)'s concept and `leastSq`'s key concept.

Use `mleLM` and `leastSq` to find the best-fit line for the same set of data. To get the datasets to match:

- `mleLM`: Click the "Make comparable to `leastSq`" checkmark. Choose $n \geq$ 25.
- `leastSq`: Double click the n slider to get the same range and increments as `mleLM`'s n slider. Ensure the random seed matches across the apps.

You can view the datasets using the "Data" tab to verify they are identical.

4. How different are the two apps' final solutions? If they are different, what might one source of that difference be?

5. *Optional Extension Q*: From a statistical standpoint, where does your similarity from (3) originate from?

6. *Optional Extension Q*: From a statistical standpoint, where does your difference from (3) originate from?

Exercise 3.4: MLE: Linear Model (Longer)

1. Explain how $y \sim \mathcal{N}(\alpha + \beta x, \sigma_u)$ translates to $\frac{1}{\sigma_u \sqrt{2\pi}} \left[\exp\left(\frac{-(y - [\alpha + \beta x])^2}{2\sigma_u^2} \right) \right]$.

2. Show that

$$\ln\left(\frac{1}{\sigma_u \sqrt{2\pi}} \left[\exp\left(\frac{-(y - [\alpha + \beta x])^2}{2\sigma_u^2} \right) \right] \right)$$

is equal to

$$-\ln(\sigma_u) - 0.5 \ln(2\pi) - \left(\frac{(y - [\alpha - \beta x])^2}{2\sigma_u^2} \right)$$

Using `mleLM`, generate a fake dataset. Set the upper-right prose style switch to "Formal," then click 👁 in the main content area.

3. Consider the (arbitrarily selected) last term in the pop-up window's two specific log-likelihood expressions, which corresponds to the dataset's last observation. Verify that the last term under the "Specific: log-likelihood expression, simplified" header is equal in value to the last term under "Specific: log-likelihood expression, unsimplified." (To verify the value you *should* obtain, go to the "Data" tab, leave the table unsorted, scroll to the last observation in the dataset, and look at the "logLH_i" column's value.)

4. Still looking at the 👁 pop-up box, consider the formula under "Generic: the log-likelihood expression." Show that another valid way of expressing this formula is

$$-n \ln(\sigma_u) - \frac{n}{2} \ln(2\pi) - \frac{1}{2\sigma_u^2} \sum_{i=1}^{n} (y_i - [\alpha + \beta x_i])^2$$

5. How does our assumption about $u \sim \mathcal{N}$ give rise to the classic linear model's likelihood expression? *(Hint: there is a connection between u's and y's distribution.)*

6. *Optional Extension Q*: In the app's generic log-likelihood expression, we could omit the $-0.5 \ln (2\pi)$ term, and we would still obtain the same parameter estimates as before (see demo below, if desired). Why?

────────────────────── **MLE lnL Equiv. Expression Demo** ──────────────────────

```
# ** Written for >=R 4.0 **
library(stats4)
data(mtcars)

# (1) Load the four functions in mleLM's globalPt_mlOptimFunc.R file
source("globalPt_mlOptmFunc.R") # if saved in current WD
    # lnL expression = function's last line

# (2) Then:
## Variant 1
LM_mll # to print the lnL expression for viewing
mod1 <- mle(LM_mll(mpg ~ wt, data=mtcars), lower=c(-Inf, -Inf, 0.0001));
summary(mod1)

## Variant 2
LM_mll2 # to print the lnL expression for viewing
mod2 <- mle(LM_mll2(mpg ~ wt, data=mtcars), lower=c(-Inf, -Inf, 0.0001));
summary(mod2)

## Variant 3
LM_mll3 # to print the lnL expression for viewing
mod3 <- mle(LM_mll3(mpg ~ wt, data=mtcars), lower=c(-Inf, -Inf, 0.0001));
summary(mod3)

## Variant 4
LM_mll4 # to print the lnL expression for viewing
mod4 <- mle(LM_mll4(mpg ~ wt, data=mtcars), lower=c(-Inf, -Inf, 0.0001));
summary(mod4)
```
────────────────────── **MLE lnL Equiv. Expression Demo** ──────────────────────

4 Linear Model Assumptions

Section 4 focuses on basic linear regression, a staple of most social science undergraduate and graduate programs. Linear regression serves as the motivation for more complex regression models, as well as the reference point for interpreting these more complex models, making linear regression's ins and outs another topic where deepening students' understanding can have big payoffs later.

4.1 Section's App Overview

4.1.1 Descriptions

This section's activities involve two major apps. Both involve simulations:

- `olsApp` (Sect. 4.3) [https://bit.ly/33IXQN5]: A multipart app that explores the ramifications of violating the Gauss–Markov assumptions for OLS estimates, as well as the normally distributed error assumption (collectively, the "classic linear regression" [CLR] assumptions). For each violation, the app executes Monte Carlo simulations using a DGP whose parameter values are selected by the student. Among other things, `olsApp` reports the simulation results, as well as various diagnostic plots for each individual simulation draw.
- `linRegEstms` (Sect. 4.4) [https://bit.ly/2YCij3g]: A variant of `olsApp`, focusing on efficiency. It compares the performance of different estimators in the presence of various CLR assumption violations.

4.1.2 Major Points

You can use these apps to demonstrate the following points. The list is not exhaustive. For a more detailed discussion of an app's features, refer to the relevant section noted above. Section 4.5 sketches out two repeatable activities that can be applied to any violation, as well as two one-off activities involving the concepts that appear in the repeatables.

- Our textbook definition of estimate bias is $E\left(\hat{\beta}\right) \neq \beta$. Simulations help concretize what that means.

  ❯ `olsApp` ▶ "No Violation," run a set of simulations. Make note of the values in the top two rows of the processed results table. They will approximately match for all estimates. Then, choose a violation from "Endogeneity" (other than "Meas. Err.: y"), run a set of simulations. Compare the top two rows again—they will not match for all estimates.

  ❯ Same as before, only have students also interact with the "Raw Simulation Output" tab, either by (a) examining the tab and being prompted to describe what each row and column in the table represents and/or (b) downloading the raw simulation results and calculating the estimates' means themselves.

- An individual estimate is not unbiased. However, the average of many such estimates, produced by an estimator, can be.

  ❯ `olsApp` ▶ "No Violation," run a set of simulations. Navigate to the "Raw Simulation Output" tab. Each row represents a set of estimates from one sampled dataset. Taking β_1 as an example, any one sample's $\hat{\beta}_1$ is quite clearly not equal to β_1. Averaging $\hat{\beta}_1$ across all the samples, though, is equal (approximately, and would be outright if we could infinitely sample).

- Gauss–Markov violations affecting efficiency matter little if your interest is good predictions of y (provided the violations are not symptoms of a more serious issue; they are not symptoms in olsApp).

> olsApp ▶ "Errors," choose any violation. Run a set of simulations. Navigate to "True y vs. $\hat{y}$" tab, pick any draw, compare dashed (true) versus solid (predicted) lines – they will be virtually identical.

- OLS is a consistent estimator: its variance gets smaller as n increases.

  > olsApp ▶ "No Violation," set $n = 150$ (or some number on the lower end of the n slider's default range), run a set of simulations. Screenshot the processed results table. Bump $n = 950$ (or some number on the n slider's higher end), keeping all other settings the same. Run a second set of simulations. Compare the processed results table to the screenshotted table – the estimated SE will be smaller from second.

  (This first bullet above emphasizes the* estimated *SE, also known as the model-based SE, to be contrasted with the next two bullets.)*

  > Same as above, only navigate to "Estimates: Distribution Plots" after the two simulation runs and select the same parameter. Screenshot the histogram from the first run, compare to the second – the histogram's spread will be smaller in second run.

  > Same as the second bullet, but instead use the estimates' CIs in the "Main" tab's processed result table – the CIs will be narrower for the second run.

  (The second and third bullets above emphasize the* "theoretical" *SE, also known as the empirical SE. There is no real substantive difference between "theoretical" and estimated SE values for the no-violation case, but that will not always be true.)*

- When n is small and the normality assumption is suspect for the population error terms, an OLS estimate's simulated sampling distribution may not be normally distributed...

  > olsApp ▶ "Normality" ▶ "Heavy-Tailed Errors," set t degrees of freedom to 3. Double click the n slider to enable smaller n possibilities than the default, set $n = 10$. Run a set of simulations. Navigate to "Estimates: Distribution Plots," compare smoothed kernel (solid blue) to normal distribution (dashed red). (Pick one of the β graphs; they tend to be the most straightforward to check.) The two lines will have a similar shape, but the dashed red line will have thicker tails than the solid blue one.

- ...but asymptotic normality can kick in quickly, depending on how nonnormal the true population errors are.

  > Same as above, except set t degrees of freedom to 20 ($n = 10$, still). Navigate to "Estimates: Distribution Plots," compare smoothed kernel (solid

blue) to normal distribution (dashed red). The estimate sampling distributions will better approximate normal than those from the previous bullet, even though n is the same.

❯ Contrast with the same $t_{df} = 3$ scenario as above, but $n = 25$. Navigate to "Estimates: Distribution Plots," compare smoothed kernel (solid blue) to normal distribution (dashed red). The estimate sampling distributions will now better approximate normal versus the $n = 10$, $t_{df} = 3$ sampling distributions.

- The apps can show what the textbook diagnostic plots for any of the various OLS violations look like, both in the presence and absence of the violation
  ❯ olsApp, pick a violation, run a set of simulations. Navigate to "Residuals: Distribution Plots," select the appropriate plot from the drop-down box (as well as your preferred type of residuals). Can contrast with the same plot's appearance for the no-violation scenario or other violations.

- Usually implicit in our discussion of estimated standard errors (which involve $\hat{\sigma}_u^2$, the estimated error variance) is whether they are unbiased estimates of an estimate's true dispersion (which involves σ_u^2, the true error variance). Again, simulations can help make this idea concrete.
  ❯ linRegEstms ▶ "No Violation," run a set of simulations, look at the "OLS" column in the processed results table. "Estimated SE (Mean)" represents the model-based standard error – the value returned in the model output by the estimator. The bottom row, "StDev of Estimate," is the empirical standard error, calculated as the slope estimate's standard deviation across all the simulations, serving as the rough "true" value of the estimate's dispersion. If the SE estimate is unbiased, the two values will approximately match for all estimates.

- Estimator A is more efficient than estimator B if trace(VCE$_A$) < trace(VCE$_B$).[33]
  ❯ linRegEstms ▶ "Errors" ▶ "Heteroscedasticity," run a set of simulations. Navigate to "Efficiency Check" tab. Select "WLS" for Model A and "OLS" for Model B – WLS's trace will be smaller than OLS's trace.
  ❯ Same general idea, except have students calculate the traces manually from either (a) the displayed matrices on the "Efficiency Check" tab or (b) downloading the simulation output from the "Raw Simulation Output" tab and manually calculating the trace (by squaring all the standard errors – all we

---

[33] There are four other mathematically equivalent ways to define efficiency (Kennedy, 2003, 37–39). For multidimensional estimators, keep in mind that A being more efficient than B does not necessarily mean A's standard errors will always be smaller than B's SEs *for every estimate.*

need to calculate the trace, since it only involves the VCE's main diagonal – then averaging appropriately).

• Robust SEs and heteroscedasticity- and autocorrelation-consistent (HAC) SEs are consistent, but not unbiased.

> linRegEstms ▶ "No Violations," set $n = 20$. Run simulations, look at processed results table for arbitrary estimate and make note of the values for "Estimated SE (Mean)" in the first three columns (the last two will be smaller than the first). Then, set $n = 400$, run an additional set of simulations, look at the same cells in the same table for the same arbitrary estimate. All three values will be equal or nearly so.

(Note: robust and HAC SEs aren't appropriate to use for inference, here, because the issues they address aren't present in the data. We're using no violations to illustrate consistency only.)

• Provided the weighting scheme is correct, WLS is BLUE in the presence of heteroscedasticity...

(uses the empirical SE/"theoretical" SE as a stand-in for the true variance/SE [= what the BLUE proofs technically use])

> linRegEstms ▶ "Heteroscedasticity," run a set of simulations. "StDev of Estimate" for WLS will be the smallest of all the unbiased linear estimators (linear = tagged with green in table key, and all four linear estimators happen to be unbiased).

• ...and its more general variant, GLS, is BLUE in the presence of autocorrelation (AC), provided the AC correction matches the true AC process.

(uses the empirical SE as a stand-in for the true variance/SE [= what the BLUE proofs technically use])

> linRegEstms ▶ "Autocorrelation," run a set of simulations. "StDev of Estimate" for GLS will be the smallest of all the linear estimators (linear = tagged with green in table key; all four linear estimators happen to be unbiased).

• When all the GMT assumptions are met *and* the population errors are normally distributed, OLS is not just the best linear unbiased estimator (BLUE), but also the best unbiased estimator (BUE).

> linRegEstms ▶ "No Violations." All the estimators are unbiased (in the slopes), but only OLS, FGLS, M.estm, and LTS end up being relevant.[34] Look at the "StDev of Estimate" row. OLS will have the smallest value across the aforementioned four columns. (If it does not, fall back to the

---

[34] The issues to which robust SEs and HAC SEs pertain aren't present in the data, making them inappropriate. The app's WLS estimate weights by $|x|^{-1}$, which is also inappropriate, as the errors aren't heteroscedastic at all for this scenario, let alone in x.

technical definition of efficiency for multidimensional estimators: on the "Efficiency Check" tab, ensure the app is displaying the "theoretical" VCEs, then compare OLS's trace to the other models' traces; OLS's trace will be the smallest.)

- Robust estimators do a better job at recovering covariate effect estimates when the population errors are appreciably non-normal.

  > `linRegEstms` ▶ "Normality" ▶ "Skewed Errors," choose χ^2 with 10 degrees of freedom. Run the simulations; M.estm and LTS will both have slope estimates closer to the truth than OLS. LTS's performance will become more OLS-like as the percentage of kept observations increases (higher values of "LTS: n to Keep" slider).

4.2 Introductory Remarks

4.2.1 Generalities

Monte Carlo simulations are a dual-edged sword for teaching econometrics, depending on the level at which the course is pitched. Pedagogically, simulations are useful because they show how an estimator performs under conditions that you, as the user, control, akin to conducting an experiment.[35] The downside is some students may get bogged down in trying to understand what every line of code is doing (or what code to write) instead of focusing on the output and thinking about what it means.

Using Monte Carlo simulations to help teach regression is not new, but using Shiny to facilitate it is. It removes the need for students to be aware of the simulation code – or to program in R at all, for non-R courses. Instead, students can focus on the pedagogically salient points.

4.2.2 Own Class Usage Examples

Undergraduate. My undergrad lecture focuses strictly on basic Gauss–Markov. I streamline `olsApp` by temporarily deactivating the "Normality," "Simultaneity," and measurement error pages. Depending on the student makeup in a given semester, I may also deactivate the fifth tab ("True y vs. $\hat{y}$"), if not also the fourth ("Residuals: Distribution Plots") on the remaining pages. We eventually articulate the assumptions as (1) $E(u|X) = 0$, (2) $\text{Corr}(u, x) = 0$ for all $x \in X$, (3) no autocorrelation, (4) no heteroscedasticity, and (5) the DGP being linear in parameters.

Earlier in the semester, students run small Monte Carlo simulations by hand using Excel for the sampling distribution lecture. From this, they get a basic

---

[35] Carsey and Harden (2013, 3–7) draw the same parallel.

grasp of what simulations involve and a more concrete sense of what sampling distributions are.

For the Gauss–Markov lecture, students receive an opening worksheet when they arrive that day. I give a 1–3-minute lead-in before having them do an opening activity with the worksheet. The worksheet is filled with regression tables whose true DGPs are plagued by various Gauss–Markov violations, with one violation appearing per table along with a variant of the same DGP with no violations as a point of comparison. Students are put into five groups, one for each table, and asked whether their table's *coefficients* or its *standard errors* seem to be affected most by the violation. Thinking in coefficient/standard error terms segues into the lecture proper, which opens with a discussion of finite-sample estimator properties. The lecture then proceeds as usual and draws parallels back to the opening activity as appropriate. Students use `olsApp` to complete a small activity, either during the lecture or as homework, depending on how long class sessions are. The activity helps to solidify what they just heard and to tie things back to the opening activity's worksheet. The instructions they receive for that activity are a toned-down version of Exercise 4.3:

Your task:

1. Pick values for n, α, β_1, and β_2 in the "No Violations" scenario. You should feel free to change the sliders from their default values. Click "Simulate!" Screenshot your results.
2. Pick one of the five OLS violations at the top of the screen. Use the same values from your "No Violations" scenario for random seed, number of simulations, n, α, β_1, and β_2. If there are additional settings for the violation you've chosen, pick whatever values you like. Click "Simulate!" Screenshot your results.

Create a new post in the Blackboard forum for this specific lecture. Your post should contain:

- Your "No Violations" screenshot.
- Your violation screenshot, for whichever scenario you chose.
- If your scenario's assumption is violated, what should the ramifications be? (1 sentence)
- Where are these ramifications evident in your simulation results? Be specific. (1–2 brief sentences)

[Note: If the activity is done during lecture, students are put into pairs or triplets and told that I will be asking them about these things in our post-activity discussion. They do not need to post anything to Blackboard.]

Graduate, Basic Regression. My graduate-level methods classes meet twice a week for 75 minutes. Students are first given the link to olsApp before the lecture on finite-sample estimator properties. They are told to spend at least 5 minutes poking around the app because we will be using it (and a more advanced version of it) multiple times during the semester. They are also told to review their notes on sampling distributions.

For the lecture itself, we go through the usual for pre-class activities (see p. 6), using the discussion as the ramp into a review of sampling distributions. What a sampling distribution *is*, in slightly more concrete terms, comes up, leading us into a very *brief* discussion of what Monte Carlo simulations are (we discuss how to run them in R/Stata in another course), and then what the app is doing; the discussion segment's ending punchline revolves around the "Estimates: Distribution Plots" tab. I move next to discussing bias and use olsApp's first two tabs throughout, making sure students have a very general feel for what the app does and what the evidence of "bias" looks like. I discuss efficiency next, at which point I switch to linRegEstms, taking care to emphasize linRegEstms has the same basic idea as olsApp, but with some extra features. We go through what evidence of "relative efficiency" looks like, ultimately leading us to wrap up with a discussion about the "best" part of BLUE. At the end of the lecture, I assign students Exercise 4.2, Q4 for the next class, which is usually the lecture on asymptotic properties. They are also told to fiddle with both apps a little more, now that they have more information about what the apps do and a better idea of how we will be using them.

The asymptotics lecture unfolds much the same as the finite-sample lecture. I use olsApp to discuss consistency, asymptotic normality, and (if we cover it) asymptotic unbiasedness, and use linRegEstms for asymptotic efficiency (if we cover it). I assign Exercise 4.1 and the rest of 4.2 as problem set questions.

After the asymptotics lecture, we move into the individual lecture sets on each CLR assumption. Students are given variants of Exercise 4.3 as a regular pre-class exercise for the first lecture in a set. There are sometimes additional, small pre-class activities asking the students to work (what ends up being) a small piece of the relevant math in a simpler context, before we encounter it in a regression setting. Each of those lectures starts and unfolds per the usual for pre-class activities (see p. 6).

4.3 The App: olsApp [https://bit.ly/33IXQN5]

olsApp is organized around four major categories of assumption violations:

1. Endogeneity *{Gauss–Markov}*
   - $E(u) \neq 0$

Figure 4.1 `olsApp`, general structure.
Package version: `shiny_1.4.0.2`

- Omitted Variable Bias
- Simultaneity Bias
- Measurement Error
  - In x (a violation)
  - In y (not a violation, given how the app induces it)
2. Errors *{Gauss–Markov}*
- Heteroscedasticity
- Autocorrelation
3. Nonlinear in Parameters *{Gauss–Markov}*
4. Normality [of Error Term] *{in least squares, needed for inference only}*
- Heavy-Tailed Errors
- Skewed Errors
- Multimodal Errors

The different assumption violations are arrayed across the top of the app as different pages. There are 12 pages in total. Each scenario contains either no violations (the default) or one violation only.

4.3.1 "Main" Tab

Common There are several input widgets common to all 12 pages:

- RANDOM SEED: Allows students to replicate their results across app sessions. Additionally, during the same app session, using the same seed for every page guarantees the only difference between "No Violations" and the selected violation is the violation itself, if all other sliders have the same values.
- # OF SUBJECTS: n, the number of observations being pulled from the population in each sample. Double clicking this slider shifts its minimum and maximum to smaller, finer-grained values, to help illustrate OLS's asymptotic properties. Double clicking again returns the slider's scale back to the default.
- # OF SIMULATIONS: the number of samples to pull from the population (S, in some of the later discussion here)
- INTERCEPT (α): the (arbitrary) true value of α in the population

Figure 4.2 `olsApp`, Results from "No Violations" ▶ "Main" tab.
Package version: `shiny_1.4.0.2`

- x's COEFF (β_1): the (arbitrary) true value of β_1 in the population
- z's COEFF (β_2): the (arbitrary) true value of β_2 in the population
- u's NOISE (σ): u's standard deviation in the population (notated as σ_u in the estimation method apps). Higher values mean u's values are more dispersed from u's mean, and therefore, observed y will contain more random noise.

Clicking **Simulate!** will run the simulations. The results are processed and displayed in the "Main" tab's main content area on the right. Each of the table's columns represents a parameter (Fig. 4.2). The table has six rows:

1. "**True Value**": A reminder of the parameter's true value for this set of simulations
2. "Estimated Value (Mean)": The parameter estimate's mean value for the S simulation draws

3. "Lower 95% CI": The lower, percentile-based 95 percent confidence interval for the S simulation draws
4. "Upper 95% CI": The upper, percentile-based 95 percent confidence interval for the S simulation draws
5. "Estimated SE (mean)": The model-based standard error, equal to the mean of the estimate's standard errors for the S simulation draws
6. "StDev of Estimate": The empirical standard error, equal to the estimate's standard deviation for the S simulation draws

   Under the processed results table, ⬇ Download a Fake Dataset allows students to save a fake dataset to their computer characterized by their specified DGP and selected CLR violation.

Violation-Specific Depending on the violation, there will be additional widgets in the left sidebar. They always appear at the top in a darker gray rectangle, underneath 🗋 No Violation Scenario :

1. Endogeneity
   - $E(u) \neq 0$: u's true mean
   - Omitted Variable Bias: degree of correlation between x and z
     ** NOTE: this page can also be used to demonstrate (1) multicollinearity's effect (set $|\mathrm{Corr}(x, z)|$ to 0.85–0.99) and (2) the effect of omitting a variable correlated with y, but not x ($\beta_2 \neq 0$ and $\mathrm{Corr}(x, z) = 0$). (To see the effect of including a completely irrelevant variable, go to "No Violations" and set $\beta_2 = 0$.)
   - Simultaneity Bias: the four parameter values for x's DGP (intercept, z's effect, the instrument's effect, y's effect on x). (The error variances, σ_y and σ_x, are constrained to be 1, to speed up the data generation.)
   - Measurement Error, both x and y: amount of measurement error as proportion of the variable's standard deviation. The measurement error is uncorrelated with the variable's true value, giving rise to biased estimates for x measurement error but not y measurement error.
2. Errors
   - Heteroscedasticity: *no additional widgets*. (The error is heteroscedastic with x, always.)
   - Autocorrelation: the autocorrelation's type (AR vs. MA), the AC coefficient. (The process is restricted to be stationary and its order is held at 1.)
3. Nonlinear in Parameters: *no additional widgets*. (The true DGP is always $y = \exp(XB + \sigma u)$.)

4. Normality [of Error Term]

- Heavy-Tailed Errors: degrees of freedom for t distribution ($u \sim t_{df}(0, 1)$). Clicking ❓ will show a small pop-up comparing t_{df} to the normal distribution.

- Skewed Errors: u's distribution (χ^2 OR skewed normal), relevant skew parameter given selected distribution. Clicking ❓ will show a small pop-up comparing the selected distribution + its skew parameter value to the normal distribution.

- Multimodal Errors: u's number of modes. u is subsequently generated as an equal mixture of that many normal distributions, each with its own mean and standard deviation. u is then centered at zero before being used in the DGP.

4.3.2 "Raw Simulation Output" Tab

Students can see the estimates of $\hat{\alpha}$, $\hat{\beta}_1$, and $\hat{\beta}_2$ from every sample on this tab. The raw results are displayed as a spreadsheet-like table in which each row represents a set of regression results from one sample. Students can export the raw results to a CSV file using ⬇ Download Results , located above the table.

4.3.3 "Estimates: Distribution Plots" Tab

This tab displays the sampling distributions of $\hat{\alpha}$, $\hat{\beta}_1$, or $\hat{\beta}_2$ as a histogram. The kernel density also appears (blue solid line), as does the normal distribution for reference (red dashed line). The rug plot along the plot's bottom provides more fine-grained information about how many values fall within each histogram bin.

4.3.4 "Residuals: Distribution Plots" Tab

The "Residuals: Distribution Plots" tab allows students to view a number of OLS diagnostic plots involving $\hat{u}$, the residual. The available plots appear in the "Plot Type" dropdown in the left sidebar. The app stores the regular, standardized, and Studentized residuals for every simulation draw. In the main content area on the right, students use the "Select Simulation Draw" slider to choose the draw, and then the "Select Residual Type" selector buttons to display the residual type of interest for the selected plot. For the plots where the residuals' distribution is being compared to some reference distribution, the type of residual dictates which reference distribution appears:

- Regular OR standardized residuals: normal distribution

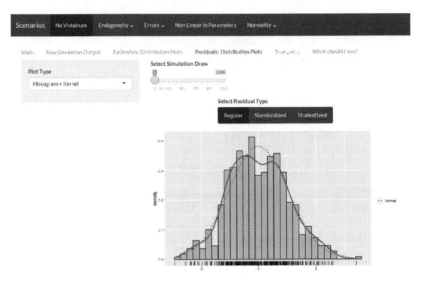

Figure 4.3 `olsApp`, "No Violations" ▶ "Residuals: Distribution Plots" tab.
Package version: `shiny_1.4.0.2`

- Studentized residuals: t distribution with $n-k-2$ degrees of freedom (where k = number of regressors)

On the whole, students can view six different plots:

1. "Histogram + Kernel": displays a histogram + kernel + reference distribution + rug plot, like the "Estimates: Distribution Plot" tab does, except it displays the draw's selected residuals instead of a parameter's simulation estimates.
2. "Q-Q Plot": displays quantiles for the selected residuals versus the residuals' corresponding reference distribution. Also overlays 95 percent pointwise confidence bands based on CIs from the reference distribution to help emphasize significant deviations.
3. "P-P Plot": same as "Q-Q Plot," only for standardized probabilities, and with pointwise bootstrapped confidence bands.
4. "Resids vs. Predictor": the usual plot to detect heteroscedastic errors, with a covariate or $\hat{y}$ on the horizontal axis and the selected residuals on the vertical axis. Students can select whether x, z, or $\hat{y}$ appears on the horizontal axis using the special selector buttons that appear to the right of the simulation draw slider for this plot type only.

5. "Autocorrelation Function": displays the autocorrelation function for the selected residuals, with number of time periods back on the horizontal axis.[36]

6. "Partial AC Function": same as above, only for partial autocorrelation.

4.3.5 "True y vs. ŷ" Tab

Whether practitioners use regression for explanatory or predictive purposes varies across the social sciences. olsApp's strong focus on all the CLR assumptions makes it oriented toward explanation – our interest is in obtaining unbiased, efficient estimates of x's effect. However, the CLR assumptions become less relevant if the practitioners' interest is predictive. The interest is now getting the most accurate y prediction possible, and if the best predictive specification involves biased individual coefficient estimates, so be it.

This tab provides an opening to discuss prediction versus explanation. It features a descriptive graph involving observed y and $\hat{y}$ for a given draw (selected using the "Select Simulation Draw" slider). The tab's scatterplot displays the selected draw's dataset, with x on the horizontal axis and y on the vertical axis (black points).[37] The app overlays y's true value given x (orange dashed line) and the model's $\hat{y}$ (teal solid line). Mousing over any data point displays observation i's true y value, i's observed y value (true + noise), and the model's predicted y_i, as well as i's (observed) x value. For "Endogeneity" ▶ "Meas. Err: x," the mouseover also displays true x's value.

4.3.6 "What should I see?" Tab

The final tab provides students with the main takeaway for the selected violation, with a focus on finite-sample properties. It provides a brief synopsis of the violation, the ramifications of violating it, and where students should look to see these ramifications in the "Main" tab's processed results table.

This tab also speaks of the OLS estimates' *efficiency* for several violations. olsApp cannot speak to efficiency directly because it involves OLS's performance with respect to *other estimators*. The app does offer some very rough heuristic comparisons, with a strong emphasis on *very*. This inability to speak to efficiency properly gives rise to this section's other main app, linRegEstms.

While this tab focuses on finite-sample properties, olsApp can also (begin to) speak to asymptotic properties. On the "Main" tab, students would need to

---

[36] "Time" amounts to the observations' order in the dataset. The "Errors" ▶ "Autocorrelation" tab uses the same fake time ordering to induce AC.

[37] The plot uses x because it is the implicit covariate of interest across all scenarios.

hold all factors constant – the violation, seed, and true parameter values – but vary the "# of Subjects (n)" slider. The most pertinent comparisons are now the simulation results from each run in which n varies. Having students screen-shot the tables can help facilitate these comparisons, because a tab's previous results will get overwritten when students change the n and run a new batch of simulations.

4.4 The App: `linRegEstms` [https://bit.ly/2YCij3g]

`olsApp` alludes to an estimator's efficiency, but to demonstrate efficiency con-cretely, you need to juxtapose one estimator's estimates with those from several other estimators. `olsApp` focuses solely on OLS, and thus, is incapable of pro-viding these comparisons. Adding other estimators to `olsApp` is doable, but also adds another layer of complexity to an already complex app.

`linRegEstms` is a variant of `olsApp` whose primary purpose is to help facil-itate discussions about efficiency. It does so by comparing OLS's performance to that of other estimators for all of the `olsApp`'s CLR violations (Fig. 4.4). Using the app to definitively establish that an estimator is *most* efficient would involve elucidating *every* possible competing estimator – a practically impos-sible task. Instead, the app focuses on some common estimators to convey *relative* efficiency's general intuition using OLS.

`linRegEstms` features five unique estimators, plus two additional OLS variants:

1. OLS
2. OLS with robust standard errors
3. OLS with heteroscedasticity- and autocorrelation-consistent (HAC) stan-dard errors, also sometimes called Newey–West standard errors
4. One of two generalized least squares (GLS) variants:
   (a) For all violations except autocorrelation: Weighted least squares via `lm()`, with weights equal to $|x|^{-1}$ (the heteroscedasticity's true form on the "Errors" ▶ "Heteroscedasticity" tab)
   (b) Autocorrelation: Generalized least squares via `lm()`, using the autocor-relation coefficient's true value for the transformations of y and X. We never know the AC coefficient's value in truth, leading to our use of FGLS in applied work (see next estimator).
5. Feasible generalized least squares (FGLS)
   (a) For all violations except autocorrelation: FGLS using `lm()`, with weights equal to $1/\exp(\hat{y}_{aux})$. The auxiliary regression uses $\ln(\hat{u}^2)$ as its dependent variable and x and z as regressors, where the $\hat{u}$s are the residuals from the original basic OLS model `lm(y ~ x + z)`.

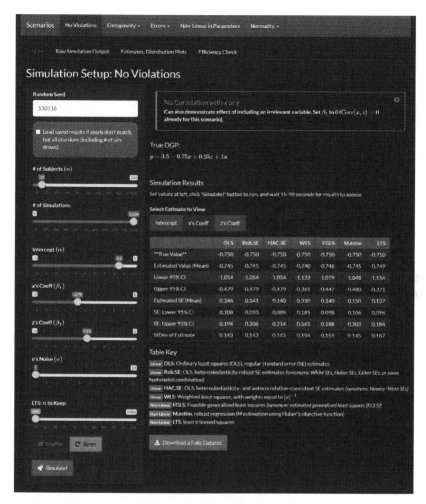

Figure 4.4 `linRegEstms`, Results from "No Violations" ▶ "Main" tab.
Package version: `shiny_1.4.0.2`

   (b) Autocorrelation: FGLS with an AR(1) error process [`nlme` package, `gls()`]

6. Robust regression (*M* estimator using Huber's objective function) [`MASS` package, `rlm()`]
7. Least trimmed squares (LTS), where the "LTS: *n* to Use" slider sets the percentage of observations whose $\hat{u}$ values LTS should use during estimation [`robustbase` package, `ltsReg()`]

   Figure 4.4 shows `linRegEstms`'s "Main" tab after running a set of simulations. Its layout and features are very similar to `olsApp`. As the figure shows, the "Main" tab still features the processed simulation results, but the table's layout has shifted to emphasize this app's specific focus. Each column now represents the output from *a specific estimator*. Users can cycle through the estimates for α, β_1, and β_2 using the "Select Estimate to View" buttons directly above the table. Below the table, the app displays a description of all the table's estimators, as well as whether or not the estimator belongs to the class of linear estimators (those of the form $\beta = My$, where M's value depends on the covariates, but not y).

The simulations take longer to run than those from olsApp because of linRegEstms's additional estimators. Accordingly, the app comes with pre-run simulation results for the default slider and random seed values for $n = \{50, 100, 500\}$. If users request a simulation scenario not in memory, the app will run the simulations, then save the results for future requests, but only if the app is run through via any means *but* Binder.[38] Users can check the "Load saved results..." checkbox below the random seed widget to permit the app to load existing results in which the scenario matches in all respects except for the seed.

Aside from the shift in focus, the other differences between linRegEstms and olsApp are trivial:

1. The "Main" tab's processed results table has two additional rows with information about the model-based standard error's confidence intervals, to illustrate whether the estimator is providing an unbiased SE estimate.

2. There are no "Residuals: Distribution Plots" and "True y vs. $\hat{y}$" tabs, mostly to lighten the server load, and because olsApp already contains the OLS versions of these plots for the same set of violations.

3. The "Estimates: Distribution Plots" tab displays a multipanel graph for the sampling distribution of a particular estimate, with each panel corresponding to an estimator. There are buttons to select which estimate's sampling distribution to view, same as on the "Main" tab.

4. The "Efficiency Check" tab compares the average variance–covariance matrix (VCE) across all the simulation draws for two estimators.[39] A set of selector buttons permits students to select either the "theoretical" VCE or the estimated VCE (Figure 4.5). The "theoretical" VCE computes the variances and covariances among all the estimator's simulated coefficient estimates (a.k.a., the empirical SE, if we spoke of the diagonal only). Doing so serves as an approximation of an estimator's true theoretical VCE – what

---

[38] Binder has no write privileges back to the GitHub repo, where the saved results would need to be stored. The results from Code Ocean runs do get saved, but the saved results do not propagate through to other users' cloned linRegEstms capsules. This save functionality produces the largest benefits when the app is hosted on a standard Shiny server (shinyapps.io or own Shiny server).

[39] Least trimmed squares is not a selectable estimator on this tab because LTS has no simple formula for its standard errors. Consequently, there is no variance–covariance matrix to extract easily from the model object.

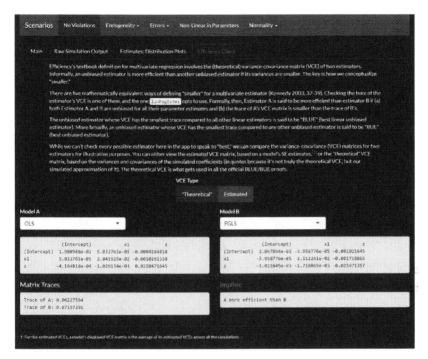

Figure 4.5 `linRegEstms`, Results from "No Violations" ▶ "Efficiency Check" tab.
Package version: `shiny_1.4.0.2`

BLUE/BUE proofs technically use. The quotation marks around "theoretical" are intended to reinforce the approximation aspect.[40] The estimated VCE option uses `vcov()` to pull all the draws' model-based VCE matrices, then averages them. For whichever of the VCE possibilities the student selects, the tab also reports the trace of each estimator's selected VCE matrix to speak to relative efficiency.

Otherwise, the apps are identical, and my previous remarks about `olsApp`'s abilities apply equally here.

4.5 Example Activities

The following example activities stem from a situation in which, across several lectures, the intended learning outcomes involve (1) students understanding sampling distributions, (2) how social scientists discuss the properties of these

---

[40] The "theoretical" VCEs for OLS, OLS with robust SEs, and OLS with HAC SEs will all be equivalent, always, because the coefficient estimates from all three models are identical.

distributions (particularly in a regression context), and (3) being able to connect these pieces of knowledge to the GMT/CLR assumptions.

4.5.1 One-Off Activities

The following activities lead students through the key statistical concepts driving Section 4.5.2's repeatable activities.

Exercise 4.1: Finite-Sample Properties

1. An estimator's properties pertain to estimate sampling distributions. What is a sampling distribution? What distinguishes it from a variable distribution?

2. What are the two finite-sample properties of estimators we discuss most often? Define each.

3. Discuss (2)'s finite-sample properties in the context of sampling distributions. For each property, draw one figure that illustrates what the property's presence and absence look like to help support your answer.

Exercise 4.2: Asymptotic Properties

1. (Exercise 4.1, Q1, if not assigned previously.)

2. What are three asymptotic properties of estimators we discuss most often? Define each.

3. Discuss (2)'s asymptotic properties in the context of sampling distributions. For each property, draw one figure that illustrates what the property's presence and absence look like to help support your answer.

4. In the app, varying the value of which slider allows us to speak broadly to asymptotics?

4.5.2 Repeatable Activities

There are two generic sets of activities that can be adapted to any of the violations ("[VIOLATION NAME]" in the questions below). You can use either app for the activities, but I recommend using olsApp if your only interest is OLS (its simulations run faster than linRegEstms's). For violations involving efficiency, linRegEstms is better suited if you want to have a more formal discussion of the concept, which necessarily involves other estimators.

Exercise 4.3: Finite-Sample Properties

1. What is [VIOLATION NAME]? Copy the verbatim definition.

2. Put (1) into your own words. What are the definition's key pieces?

3. On the `olsApp`'s [VIOLATION NAME] page, examine the true DGP for [VIOLATION NAME] on the "Main" tab. How does the app induce the violation?

4. Provided there are no other assumption violations, does [VIOLATION NAME] affect OLS estimates' *biasedness* or their *efficiency*?

5. From the app's [VIOLATION NAME] page, click ▢ No Violation Scenario in the "Main" tab's left sidebar. Then, run 1000 simulations. In the tab's processed results table, which row(s) are most relevant to check, in light of your answer to (4)?

6. Using the relevant rows you indicated in (5), what would evidence of (4)'s answer look like? Is this evidence indeed present?

7. On the "Estimates: Distribution Plots" tab, where in the graph(s) is your answer to (4) evident?

8. *If violation pertains to efficiency* AND *students are using* `linRegEstms`: Same question as (7), but instead, use evidence from the "Efficiency Check" tab.

9. Which of the diagnostic plot(s) under "Residuals: Distribution Plots" can we use to detect [VIOLATION NAME]? For each plot you name, describe what the plot should look like in both [VIOLATION NAME]'s presence and its absence.

Exercise 4.4: Asymptotic Properties

1. If [VIOLATION NAME]'s effects disappear asymptotically, what does that imply we should see in our simulation results?

2. (Exercise 4.2, Q4, if not assigned previously.)

3. Using the relevant slider from (2), run three sets of simulations – one with "low" values of the slider, one with "medium," and one with "high," in relative terms. Be sure to note the results from each. Where in this output is your answer to (1) evident?

4.6 Related Apps by Others

This section focused on CLR assumption violations, but other issues can arise in linear regression that may induce the appearance of violations. Others have written apps that focus on some of these issues:

- Diagnosing functional form misspecification: https://gallery.shinyapps.io/ slr_diag/

- Diagnosing influential data points: https://omaymas.shinyapps.io/Influence_ Analysis/

5 Encore: Shrinkage Methods

The apps so far have focused on fundamentals. In this penultimate section, I showcase Shiny's abilities to help students interact with newer topics.

5.1 Section's App Overview

5.1.1 Descriptions

This section contains two apps:

1. `leastSqLASSO` (Sect. 5.3) [`https://bit.ly/37u2b7C`]: a variant of `leastSq` (Sect. 3.3), adapted for LASSO.
2. `LASSO_bchamp` (Sect. 5.4):[41] Uses replication data from Nicholas Beauchamp's "Predicting and Interpolating State-Level Polls Using Twitter Textual Data" (2017, *American Journal of Political Science*) to introduce students to LASSO models, allowing them to manually change λ's value and observe the performance of the resulting predictive model.[42] Also includes an interactive data viewer to examine word usage on a state–date basis.

5.1.2 Major Points

You can use these apps to demonstrate the following points. The list is not exhaustive. For a more detailed discussion of a given app's features, refer to the relevant subsection noted above. Section 5.5's activities focus on juxtaposing LASSO with OLS and judging a model's predictive performance.

- λ is the key new piece in LASSO. It determines the size of LASSO's penalization term...
  > `leastSqLASSO`, generate fake data, select a small λ. Pick a few arbitrary combinations of β_1 and β_2 to check, being sure to note the LASSO penalty term's size ("Main" tab, "Size of current penalty" header). Reload the app, keep seed and n the same, but choose a larger λ. Check the same β_1 and β_2 combinations again; penalty term will be larger.

---

[41] *This app cannot run on Binder because its data files are too large. However, for a stripped-down version of the app, with the analyses pre-loaded and no interactive data viewer:* [`https://bit.ly/39IQFsO`] .

[42] Franc Bracun's `LinearRegression` app (available at https://francb.shinyapps.io/Linear Regression/) also focuses on demonstrating the same types of models in a similar context, albeit using one of eight artificially generated datasets instead of real-world data.

- ...but λ's value is treated as fixed during estimation. Its value is chosen before the estimation procedure begins.
  > leastSqLASSO, generate fake data. Students are prompted to choose their λ value next, with all other content in the left sidebar hidden, reinforcing λ's before-not-during nature. After students choose a value, it stays displayed in the sidebar, to help reinforce that λ is still used during estimation.
- LASSO's loss function is very similar to OLS's. The only difference is the additional penalty term...
  > leastSqLASSO, generate fake data, and pick a λ. Switch language to "Formal", then ⊙ . The generic loss function's first line breaks the expression into its OLS and LASSO pieces.
- ...to the point where LASSO's loss function is equivalent to OLS's when $\lambda = 0$.
  > leastSqLASSO, generate fake data, set $\lambda = 0$. Perform same steps as previous point; the LASSO term will quite clearly drop out of the loss function, leaving only the OLS portion.
- Models that perform respectably in sample can perform poorly when applied out of sample.
  > LASSO_bchamp, set $\lambda = 0.15$, run the model, examine fit statistics on the "Main" tab. The in-sample R^2 is 0.56, but the out-of-sample R^2 is ≈ 0.
- More covariates in a model does not necessarily translate to better predictive power in a LASSO context.
  > LASSO_bchamp, run the previous example for $\lambda = 0.15$. Go to the "Data: Fit Stats" tab, make note of how many covariates entered the specification along with the in-sample R^2. Then, set $\lambda = 0$ to make the model equivalent to OLS and run the model again. Go to the "Data: Fit Stats" tab and compare the number of covariates for the two models, as well as their in-sample R^2s.
- Different goodness-of-fit (GoF) statistics can suggest different "best" models.
  > LASSO_bchamp, run the model for $\lambda = 0.02$. Then, click ⚔ Show Replication . Go to the "Data: Fit Stats" tab and compare GoF measures. The replication model ($\lambda = 0.001$) has the best mean squared error and R^2 (both in and out of sample), but $\lambda = 0.02$ has the best AIC and BIC (both in and out of sample).
- Higher λ values correspond to fewer regressors in the model.
  > LASSO_bchamp, run the model for $\lambda = 0.01$, then run the model again for $\lambda = 0.02$. Go to the "# Covariates" tab; $\lambda = 0.01$ has 25 covariates, while $\lambda = 0.02$ has 4.

5.2 Introductory Remarks

I use shrinkage methods – ridge regression, LASSO, elastic net – as this section's running example because of how complex these methods are, relative to more classic forms of regression. The models have new ideas that students may not have encountered in other contexts before, like hyperparameters for frequentist-trained students. Further, there are familiar ideas that appear with a new twist, like minimizing the sum of the squares, but with an additional penalty term in the expression we ultimately minimize. From a big-picture perspective, there are also new things to understand. There are several kinds of shrinkage methods, for instance, and distinguishing among them involves yet another hyperparameter.

We can use Shiny to direct our students' attention to one key idea at a time, allowing them to bracket the other new pieces that might otherwise clamor for their attention. In so doing, students can more sturdily build the conceptual foundations on which other shrinkage model concepts can rest. From facilitating those foundations, the app can then also serve as a way to frame the subsequent class discussions, at both the micro and macro levels. At a micro level, instructors can slowly layer in the other new concepts associated with shrinkage methods, using the students' work with the app to help scaffold. At a macro level, the app can set up discussions of larger econometric themes that span multiple classes of models, such as model specification, model diagnostics, and the bias–variance trade-off in estimation.

Social scientists have a particular interest in LASSO because of its ability to help guide covariate selection, stemming from how its penalty expression is constructed. This feature means we can use LASSO to help cull a large list of predictors (and those predictors' potential interactions with each other) for an outcome of interest, leaving a smaller subset of relevant covariates. This section's apps, leastSqLASSO and LASSO_bchamp, focus on LASSO alone because of the estimator's potential utility for covariate selection, but either could be tweaked to allow for other shrinkage methods like ridge regression and/or elastic net models.

The LASSO estimates for a set of data will be those that satisfy:

$$\underset{B}{\arg\min} \left\{ \underbrace{(y - XB)^2}_{\text{regular OLS}} + \underbrace{\lambda \sum_{k=1}^{K} (|\beta_k|)}_{\text{penalization}} \right\} \tag{5.1}$$

$\lambda \ (\geq 0)$ is the major hyperparameter for LASSO models – "hyper" because its value is not estimated by the model, but instead, is set by the user. λ represents the size of the LASSO penalization term (Eq. 5.1), with larger λs corresponding

LASSO: The Intuition

Figure 5.1 `leastSqLASSO`, "Main" tab.
Package version: `shiny_1.4.0.2`

to higher penalties. However, for students first learning about these models, the hyperparameter's presence marks a departure from classic regression. Our standard (frequentist) regressions are generally devoid of hyperparameters.[43] Many students will not only be learning about shrinkage methods for the first time, but will also be wrapping their minds around a new methods concept that transcends these models.

5.3 The App: `leastSqLASSO` [https://bit.ly/37u2b7C]

The `leastSqLASSO` app (Fig. 5.1) addresses how LASSO finds its best-fit line, to begin developing students' intuition about λ's role. The app's particulars are nearly identical to `leastSq`, so all of Sect. 3.3's general remarks continue to apply.

As for the differences that do exist between the two apps:

- The app uses LASSO's loss function, not OLS's.

---

[43] Students with a Bayesian background will be more familiar with the idea, as Bayesian priors play the same role.

- Between the [⊞ Generate Fake Data] and the parameter sliders, an additional segment appears for students to choose their λ value. Underneath λ's slider, a small "Wait, what's this?" link leads to a pop-up window with a brief overview of λ's role.
- The app estimates the actual LASSO model using glmnet(), which requires at least two covariates. The new, second covariate, z, is a binary variable.
- The LASSO penalty term's value, for the current β_1 and β_2 selections, is printed on the "Main" tab, above the current guess's penalized sum of squares.
- Before the data are passed to glmnet(), y, x, and z are standardized to have mean 0 and unit variance.
- There is no α slider because regressions using standardized data have an intercept of 0.
- The app's "Main" tab shows two graphs, corresponding to the two z values. The labels above the graph refer to z's unstandardized value.

leastSqLASSO's additional covariate, as well as its standardizing of the data, means its results for a given n and seed are not comparable to leastSq's for the same n/seed combination, even if leastSqLASSO's $\lambda = 0$.

5.4 The App: LASSO_bchamp[44]

Above, leastSqLASSO temporarily reduces the amount of moving parts for students to contend with, allowing them to focus on developing their intuition about λ and the role it plays. However, it has only two covariates – hardly an ideal situation for showcasing LASSO's ability to help narrow down a large list of candidate predictors. leastSqLASSO is also silent on the proposed model's predictive power.

LASSO_bchamp addresses these more applied areas by using replication data from a peer-reviewed article. Using the app, students can begin to get a better sense of (a) what a shrinkage method does, in an applied context, and (b) some criteria for evaluating whether the estimated model performs well or poorly. Using an applied substantive article brings additional benefits: students can steep themselves further in the specific language of shrinkage methods in the context of a substantive application, read about the potential costs and benefits associated with using these methods in this particular substantive application, and see the utility of these methods when brought to bear on substantive questions more broadly.

---

[44] Full-featured version runnable in Code Ocean capsule only. For stripped-down version (fn. 41): [https://bit.ly/39IQFs0].

LASSO: Beauchamp 2017

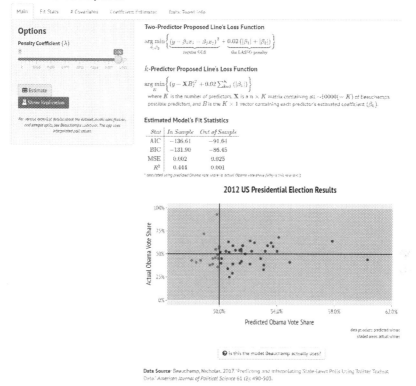

Figure 5.2 LASSO_bchamp, "Main" tab after estimating model with $\lambda = 0.02$.
Package version: shiny_1.4.0.2

Nicholas Beauchamp's (2017) interest in "Predicting and Interpolating State-Level Polls Using Twitter Textual Data" is public opinion polling data from US states. These data can be expensive to gather, making pollsters and scholars alike very interested in any technique that could approximate poll-gathered information. Beauchamp's major contribution is articulating such a technique: using geocoded Twitter data to interpolate state-level polls. He has over 120 million relevant tweets in his sample from the lead-up to the 2012 US presidential election, with approximately 10,000 possible predictors (2017, 493) – an ideal situation for shrinkage methods like LASSO.

5.4.1 "Main" Tab

LASSO_bchamp allows students to manually change λ's value using a slider and observe how the model performs (Fig. 5.2). These features appear on the

"Main" tab, in the left sidebar. Students must click ⊞ Estimate to reesti-
mate the model after changing λ, to cut down on server load. Setting $\lambda = 0$ is
equivalent to OLS, providing students with a more familiar comparison point.
When students are ready to see the λ value Beauchamp selects in the article's
actual replication files, they can click 🔨 Show Replication . Further information about the replication files, including technical information about the
dataset, appears in Beauchamp's codebook; a link to the codebook appears at
the bottom of the left sidebar.

On the right, the app outputs three chunks of information for users. It begins
by writing out LASSO's loss function, first for a simple two-predictor case
before generalizing to K predictors. In the equation, the app labels (1) the set
of terms corresponding to the usual OLS loss function and (2) the set of terms
corresponding to the LASSO penalty. The app also inserts λ's current value into
these equations. Mousing over the two-predictor case provides a small tooltip
to contextualize its inclusion.

In the next information chunk, the app provides a table with goodness-of-fit
(GoF) statistics – AIC, BIC, mean squared error, and R^2. Displaying these specific quantities stems from Beauchamp's discussion in the article, where he uses
these four measures to evaluate model performance. Also like Beauchamp, the
app calculates these four GoF statistics on two separate samples: the smaller,
initial estimation sample ("*In Sample*") and the larger, validation sample ("*Out
of Sample*"). Students can use the GoF measures to help guide their decisions
about which λ seems to produce the best-performing model. The predictions
are expressed in terms of Barack Obama's actual versus predicted share of a
state's popular vote in the 2012 US presidential election.

Students use these state-by-state predicted versus actual values to evaluate
the model's performance for each value of λ they select. While comparing predicted versus actual is *a* way to evaluate a model's predictive power, it is not the
only one. Beauchamp discusses several possibilities used by scholars to date
(2017, 491–493), with real versus actual being one example. The app provides
a small "Why is this relevant?" link below the GoF table that opens a pop-up
box to emphasize this point of Beauchamp's.

The "Main" tab's final information chunk is an interactive graph, displaying
the predicted quantities from the estimated LASSO model against the observed
state-level election results. Users can zoom the graph in and out to better examine segments of interest. Point colors represent whether the LASSO model
predicted the state to go for Obama, the 2012 Democratic candidate (blue),
or Mitt Romney, the 2012 Republican candidate (red). The plot area's background shading corresponds to actual vote share. Points appearing in the blue

LASSO: Beauchamp 2017

Main   Fit Stats   # Covariates   Coefficient Estimates   Data/Tweet Info

Choose Format

Table   Graph

shaded cells = best current value (lowest = best for all except R^2, where highest = best)
shaded row = replication

lambda	in.AIC	oos.AIC	in.BIC	oos.BIC	in.MSE	oos.MSE	in.R2	oos.R2	#Non0Bs
0.001	74.75	278.66	467.79	530.06	0.00200	0.01700	0.866	0.397	194
0.004	-35.84	22.76	39.55	105.70	0.00100	0.02000	0.876	0.243	64
0.006	-80.43	-19.86	-30.95	34.56	0.00100	0.02100	0.858	0.182	42
0.008	-96.48	-36.10	-57.61	8.66	0.00100	0.02300	0.823	0.112	33
0.01	-110.30	-50.01	-80.85	-17.62	0.00100	0.02500	0.768	0.032	25
0.013	-131.67	-75.06	-117.53	-59.51	0.00200	0.02600	0.654	0.000	12
0.02	-136.61	-91.64	-131.90	-86.45	0.00200	0.02500	0.444	0.001	4

* oos.mse is synonymous with the mean squared prediction error (MSPE).

Figure 5.3 LASSO_bchamp, "Fit Stats" tab after estimating several models, including Beauchamp's λ from his replication files. Package version: shiny_1.4.0.2

segment are states with an actual Obama majority; points in the red segment, an actual Romney majority. Users are able to mouse over each point to see which US state it represents, the model's predicted value for the state's Obama vote share, its actual Obama vote share, and whether the state appears in the estimation sample. Visually, a good-performing model will be one in which, for many points, the point color matches the graph background color.

5.4.2 "Fit Stats" Tab

On a second tab, a table displays all the λ values for which the student has estimated a model, along with the various fit statistics associated with each λ (Fig. 5.3). The table also reports the number of nonzero coefficients remaining in the model ("#Non0Bs" column); the same information appears on the "# Covariates" tab.

The "Fit Stats" tab can also display the goodness-of-fit values in an interactive graph. The graph has the same zooming and panning abilities as all the app's other graphs. Users select whether to view the table or graph using the "Choose Format" selector buttons at the top of the tab.

5.4.3 "# Covariates" Tab

The third tab displays information regarding the number of nonzero coefficients in each estimated model, either in a table or graphically (Fig. 5.4). The nonzero coefficients matter because they indicate the number of regressors the model ends up keeping, given the user's selected λ value. Like the "Fit Stats" tab, users select table versus graph using selector buttons at the tab's top. Also like

LASSO: Beauchamp 2017

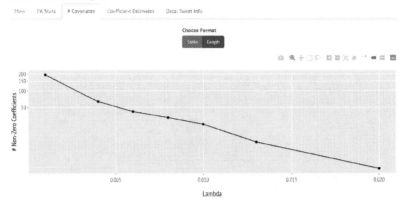

Figure 5.4 LASSO_bchamp, "# Covariates" tab after estimating several models, including Beauchamp's λ from his replication files. Package version: shiny_1.4.0.2

before, the graph has zooming and panning abilities. The information in the last column of the "Fit Stats" tab's table is identical to that in the "# Covariates" tab's table.

5.4.4 "Coefficient Estimates" Tab

The fourth tab displays the coefficient estimates for every estimated model so far (Fig. 5.5). Beauchamp's covariates represent how many times a specific word appeared in tweets from a particular date and US state, converted to a percentage of the top 10,000 words used for that state–date pair. Students use a dropdown box to select the λ corresponding to the model of interest. The table contains the unstandardized coefficients outputted by glmnet(). The table automatically puts the intercept in the first row and sorts the subsequent coefficients by their magnitude's absolute value. A search box above the table's upper-right corner allows students to search for specific words of interest.

5.4.5 "Data: Tweet Info" Tab[45]

The final tab provides users with descriptive information about Beauchamp's tweets on a state–date basis, matching his unit of analysis (Fig. 5.6). Users select the state of interest using the interactive map on the left and the date of

---

[45] This tab is unavailable in the app's lite version on Binder.

LASSO: Beauchamp 2017

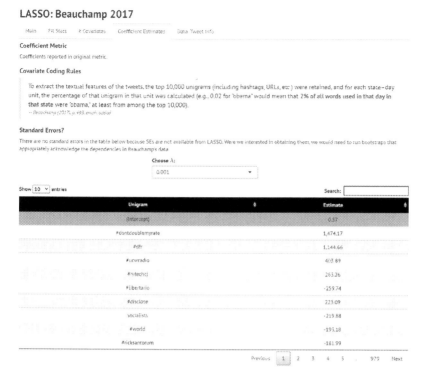

Figure 5.5 LASSO_bchamp, "Coefficient Estimates" tab for Beauchamp's λ from his replication files. Package version: `shiny_1.4.0.2`

interest using the small calendar on the right. Both the map and calendar must have a selection before the histogram will draw.

The app outputs a histogram of word frequencies, sorted from high to low, for that state on that particular day. The specific words are displayed along the horizontal axis. Users can zoom in to specific parts of the graph by dragging a selection box around the relevant portion of the plot, and can also pan to the left and right; to zoom out, double click inside the plot area. Mousing over each bar provides a tooltip with the bar's corresponding word, as well as its state–date frequency (as a percentage).

5.5 Example Exercises

The following example activities stem from a situation in which, across several lectures, the intended learning outcomes involve students (1) understanding what LASSO is, (2) being able to articulate the similarities and differences between OLS and LASSO, (3) seeing how LASSO's differences enable it

LASSO: Beauchamp 2017

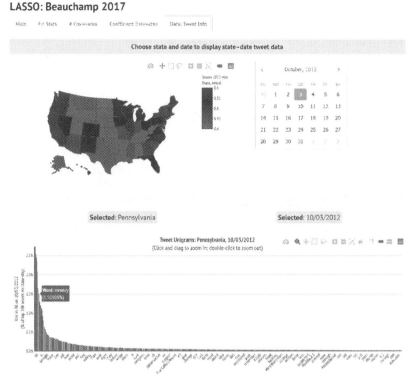

Figure 5.6 LASSO_bchamp, "Data: Tweet Info" tab.
Package version: `shiny_1.4.0.2`

to speak to variable selection, and (4) being able to assess a given model specification's predictive power.

Exercise 5.1: Pre-Class 1 (Focus: Estimation)

This question presupposes students have already experimented with `leastSq`.

1. Loss functions are a more general way to describe a particular estimation method's best-fit rule. For instance, the loss function for an OLS model with standardized coefficients would be:

$$\arg\min_{\beta_1, \beta_2}\left\{(y - \beta_1 x_1 - \beta_2 x_2)^2\right\}$$

Explain the origin of this expression. *(Hint: think back to* `leastSq`.*)*

2. Is the best-fit line the one that minimizes or maximizes the loss function's value? What leads you to this conclusion?

3. Load LASSO_bchamp and examine the first equation on the right (no need to click anything). The equation expresses LASSO's loss function.

(LASSO also standardizes its coefficients, so there is no intercept.) How is it different from OLS's loss function?

4. There is a situation in which OLS's and LASSO's loss function will be the same. What is it? Confirm it using the app.

5. What role does λ seem to play? Sketch a graph showing the relationship between its value and the loss function's overall value, holding all else equal.

6. Connect your answer for (5) back to your answer for (2).

Exercise 5.2: Pre-Class 2 (Focus: Article and LASSO Basics)

These questions presuppose students have read, or have been assigned to read, Beauchamp's original article.

1. Explain Beauchamp (2017)'s major contribution, in your own words. Be sure to note his dependent variable.

2. LASSO_bchamp focuses on LASSO models, which you can think of as "OLS models with a twist" in this context. Beauchamp discusses LASSO models on page 495, under the auspices of discussing elastic-net models, a more general model type, of which LASSO is a special case. Broadly speaking, based on Beauchamp's discussion of LASSO, what seems to distinguish LASSO models from classic OLS? Try to put it in your own words.

Load LASSO_bchamp. Experiment with the app for a few minutes, exploring its various tabs.

3. Estimate a LASSO model with $\lambda = 0.01$, temporarily putting aside whether this is a "good" model. Navigate to the "Coefficient Estimates" tab. Beauchamp's LASSO coefficients can be interpreted the same as OLS coefficients. Interpret the coefficient for #POLITICS.

4. All the substantive covariates are in the same units, making their coefficients' magnitudes comparable (Fox, 2016, 100–102). For the $\lambda = 0.01$ model, list the three covariates with the largest effects, holding all else equal.

5. How does y respond to a change in each of (4)'s three covariates, holding all else equal?

Exercise 5.3: Longer Set 1

These questions work well when paired with Exercise 5.1. They can also be modified to use leastSqLASSO more heavily, if having students work through the math once is unnecessary.

Table 5.3 Toy Data:
Standardized

x_1	x_2	y
-1.306	-0.076	-0.967
0.783	-1.286	-0.752
-0.261	0.227	0.967
0.783	1.135	0.752

1. Using Table 5.3, compute the value of OLS's loss function if $\beta_1 = 0.4$, $\beta_2 = 0.6$.

2. Do the same as (1) again, only this time, using $\beta_1 = 0.4$, $\beta_2 = 0.8$.

3. Consider your answers to (1) and (2). At the moment, which set of OLS estimates is preferable?

4. Do the same as (1), only for LASSO's loss function. Calculate it for $\lambda = 0.1$.

5. Do the same as (2), only for LASSO's loss function. Continue to use $\lambda = 0.1$.

6. Consider your answers to (4) and (5). At the moment, which set of LASSO specifications is preferable?

7. If there are differences between the best OLS versus LASSO specification, what could be a reason? Can you reformulate your reason into a broader statement about the behavior of LASSO's loss function?

8. If you changed $\lambda = 0.3$ for (4) and (5), do your conclusions from (7) change any? Can you make any additional, broad statements about the behavior of LASSO's loss function? Connect your statement back to your answer from Exercise 5.1, Q2.

9. *Optional, Aside Q*: If we added another standardized covariate to Table 5.3's model, we would run into estimation trouble. Why? *(Hint: think about how many unstandardized estimates it implies.)*

Exercise 5.4: Longer Set 2 (Focus: Prediction – Conceptual)

These questions presuppose students have read Beauchamp's original article.

1. What distinguishes using regression for predictive rather than causal purposes?

2. LASSO models do not include standard errors. We would need to take additional steps, like bootstrapping, to obtain them. Is the lack of SEs a problem?

Using LASSO_bchamp, find the λ that you believe produces the best model.

3. What criteria did you use to determine the "best" model? Justify the decision.

4. Beauchamp ends up melding together features from different models to create a more nuanced technique that he uses in the paper as his preferred model. What is the difference between that technique and a basic LASSO? What led him to create the new technique instead of using an existing one (like LASSO)?

5. We know using R^2 as a gauge of a model's predictive performance has drawbacks. What are they? Is there a viable alternative fit statistic we could use?

6. One of our fears when we are interested in prediction is overfitting a model. What is overfitting? Why is it problematic?

7. Splitting the sample into an estimation set ("in sample") and a test set ("out of sample") can help combat overfitting. How?

Exercise 5.5: Longer Set 3
Same general idea as Exercise 3.2, but for LASSO's loss function.

6 Concluding Remarks

In this Element, I have made the case for instructors to consider using Shiny to better teach econometric models to their students. Shiny makes this possible by making students more active participants in the learning process, by targeting similar concepts in different contexts, by prompting students more frequently to reflect on what they see and by representing the same information in multiple ways.

To help instructors incorporate Shiny, the Element provides six apps, with detailed documentation about their capabilities. The Element's four main apps focus on two staples of first-year PhD courses: estimating regressions and linear regression assumption violations. Two additional apps pertain to LASSO, to help showcase Shiny's ability to help make newer material more accessible. I explained the capabilities of the six apps and what instructors can show with them. I also provided a handful of example activities involving the apps, based around a particular set of learning outcomes.

In addition to providing off-the-shelf ready apps, the Element also recognizes that incorporating Shiny into one's teaching will eventually encompass topics beyond those covered here. Accordingly, I also spent time laying out how interested instructors could modify the Element apps' structure to create similarly structured apps about different topics. Section 2 discussed the apps' general structure, what some likely modifications could be, and how instructors would go about making them. The discussion does still presuppose some basic familiarity with Shiny, but the entry costs are far lower than crafting a new app from scratch, particularly since all of the major meta-level decisions about app layout and code structure have already been made.

Above all, the Element emphasizes thinking about the content we teach in new ways. I encourage instructors to turn an analytic eye toward their teaching and consider whether, where, and how Shiny can make them more effective.

Appendix A Shiny Setup Resources

A.1 Deploying Your App

If you want others to be able to run your app, you will have to deploy it. RStudio has multiple, in-depth articles about the possibilities.[46] You have three broad options:

1. **Distribute your app's raw code** for users to run locally on their own machines.
   - *Advantages*: You do not need to find a Shiny server to host your app, which also means the number of people simultaneously using the app is irrelevant.[47]
   - *Disadvantages*: Users will need to have R and shiny installed, along with any additional packages your app uses (and the correct version of those packages). Users will also have access to your app's code – not a big deal, if your code is open source, but more problematic if you would like the app's code to stay under wraps. See also footnote 49.

2. **Make your app into a package** for users to run locally on their own machines.
   - *Advantages*: As before, you do not need to find a Shiny server to host your app. The number of simultaneous users is again irrelevant. Additionally, running the app requires users to type only one line of code in the Console. Formatting the app as a package also means you are more likely to remember to declare any additional packages your app uses as dependencies, compliments of the package's DESCRIPTION file. The golem package is geared specifically toward helping users write Shiny apps to be distributed as packages.[48]
   - *Disadvantages*: As above, users will have access to your app's code. This option also still relies on the user installing (or R installing on the user's behalf) the correct package versions, but any R package faces this potential issue.[49]

---

[46] http://shiny.rstudio.com/articles/#deployment

[47] Section A.2 touches on why this may end up mattering.

[48] https://thinkr-open.github.io/golem

[49] It's possible to use a Docker container to distribute your app. Whether or not using Docker is less hassle than other possibilities for running the app locally is debatable. Users must install Docker successfully (https://docs.docker.com/install/) to run any Docker containers locally. Alternatively, you can also use Electron (https://github.com/ColumbusCollaboratory/electron-quick-start) to distribute your app as an executable file, obtaining the same functionality as a Docker container with no additional setup work needed on your users' end. If you use Electron, you will need to build separate executables for PC and Mac.

3. **Host your app remotely** on a web server.

   - *Advantages*: Your app is accessible to anyone with an internet connection. Additionally, the app's code is hidden from users unless you specify otherwise.
   - *Disadvantages*: You will need to find a server to host your app (see Sect. A.1.1's list). Depending on which option you pick, you may need to set up the server to run Shiny apps, and there may also be a small monthly cost involved for the server space. The costliness typically correlates with how much run time your app is allocated per month. You will also have to be mindful of the number of users using your app simultaneously, and making sure your app can handle the load.

   > VARIANT OF #3: Host your app remotely using a **cloud-based replication** service.

   - *Advantages*: Your app is accessible to anyone with an internet connection. You will also be able to version control both packages and R, guaranteeing your apps will always launch without issue. Further, the number of simultaneous users is irrelevant, because each app launch spins up a new mini Shiny server.
   - *Disadvantages*: Users will have access to your app's code. For some of the cloud-based replication services, users need to create a (free) account before they can execute any code, and there can be some additional clicking involved before the app launches.

A.1.1 Conventional Web Server

If you are interested in hosting your app remotely on a server, there are a couple of options. Of those that follow, shinyapps.io or Digital Ocean are two of the more common ones:

- **shinyapps.io**
  RStudio's official hosting space for Shiny apps. Can upload the app easily through shinyapps.io's integration with RStudio.
  - EASE OF SETUP: Easy
  - EASE OF USE (USER): Easy
  - LOCATION: www.shinyapps.io
  - SETUP: Create shinyapps.io account, connect to shinyapps.io account in RStudio via File ▶ Publish, upload app using the same menu option, done.

- COST: Free for five apps and up to 25 hours of run time per month. For more apps and/or more run time, see the pricing list.[50]
- NOTES: App code not visible by default, but can be enabled as an option. No educator discount available. Has defaults set to help with performance and balancing.

- **Amazon Web Services (AWS)**
  Amazon's cloud computing service. You can customize EC2 server space for any purpose, including installing a Shiny server and running Shiny apps.
  - EASE OF SETUP: Advanced
  - EASE OF USE (USER): Easy
  - LOCATION: https://aws.amazon.com
  - SETUP: Create AWS account, follow tutorial for setting up Shiny on AWS here.[51] If you want to use Docker, see instructions here.[52]
  - COST: Free for one year ("Free Tier") with 750 hours of EC2 time per month and a select-your-own amount of RAM and storage. Becomes pay as you go after 12 months.
  - NOTES: AWS Educator account available, which also provides 150 credits to use for free on AWS servers for 1 year.

- **DigitalOcean**
  Similar to AWS, cloud computing option with customizable servers. Can set up a Shiny server to run Shiny apps.
  - EASE OF SETUP: Advanced
  - EASE OF USE (USER): Easy
  - LOCATION: www.digitalocean.com
  - SETUP: Create DigitalOcean account, follow Dean Attali's tutorial[53] for the rest of the setup.
  - COST: At the time of this writing, cheapest plan is $5 per month for a server with 1 GB of RAM, 1 virtual CPU, 25 GB of disk space (SSD), and a 1 TB transfer rate. Additional pricing here[54] (see "Standard Droplets").
  - NOTES: Can upgrade to a more high-powered plan if you need more computing power, pay for the number of hours your server runs with the higher plan, and then downgrade again to a cheaper plan.

- **Own web server**
  If you own a web server and it runs Linux, you can enable it to be a Shiny server.

---

[50] https://www.shinyapps.io/#pricing
[51] https://www.r-bloggers.com/shiny-server-on-aws/
[52] https://www.bryanwhiting.com/2019/02/rshiny-on-docker-part1/
[53] https://deanattali.com/2015/05/09/setup-rstudio-shiny-server-digital-ocean/
[54] https://www.digitalocean.com/pricing/

- EASE OF SETUP: Expert
- EASE OF USE (USER): Easy
- LOCATION: Web address dependent on your server's configuration.
- SETUP: Requires that you have root access and that your server be running one of three[55] Linux distributions. You will need to install R on your server first (preferably via the Linux repository), then `shiny`, then Shiny Server.[56] Shiny Server's detailed administrator's guide is here.[57]
- COST: None additional, aside from your server's usual operating costs.
- NOTES: None.

DigitalOcean is an example of a cloud-hosting service. However, most cloud services can host a Shiny server. Linode[58] is another example (setup instructions[59]).

I suggest starting with shinyapps.io's free plan as you begin fiddling. Once you get a sense of whether Shiny can help, how you'll use the apps, which apps you'll be using, and how resource intensive the apps are, you can then look into the other possibilities to see which ones best fit your expected usage patterns and budget, if the free shinyapps.io account is insufficient.

> ⚠ If you are using a server and planning an in-class activity involving students using your app: **always do a test run beforehand**. Ensure both your app and your server can handle as many simultaneous users as you have students without lagging or crashing (which is *not* a given – see Section A.2 for more).

A.1.2 Cloud-Based Replication Service

- **Binder**
  Uses Git repositories to launch temporary web-based Jupyter, R, or Shiny sessions for any user with the Git repo's Binder URL. Works with GitHub repos that contain the necessary Binder setup files (among certain other Git/DOI sources).
  - EASE OF SETUP: Intermediate
  - EASE OF USE (USER): Easy

---

[55] https://docs.rstudio.com/shiny-server/#system-requirements
[56] https://www.rstudio.com/products/shiny/download-server/
[57] http://docs.rstudio.com/shiny-server/
[58] http://www.linode.com
[59] https://www.linode.com/docs/development/r/how-to-deploy-rshiny-server-on-ubuntu-and-debian/#what-is-shiny

- LOCATION: https://mybinder.org/
- SETUP: See the Turing Institute's Zero-to-Binder tutorial for R here.[60] In short: create public GitHub repo, define `runtime.txt` + `install.R` locally (details[61]), [62] upload all usual app files + `runtime.txt` + `install.R` to the repo, go to mybinder.org and follow the instructions on the homepage to compile the Binder,[63] distribute the Binder URL to others, done.
- COST: Free. (App session will terminate after $\sim$10 minutes of inactivity or $\sim$12 hours after instantiation.)
- NOTES: App code will be visible. Permits $\sim$50–100 simultaneous users. The Binder's initial compile can take a while (see fn. 65). See also the official Binder–R examples.[64]

- **Code Ocean**
  Website that permits users to upload code, designed to promote transparent, replicable research. Its interactive RStudio environment can run Shiny apps.
  - EASE OF SETUP: Intermediate
  - EASE OF USE (USER): Intermediate
  - LOCATION: www.codeocean.com
  - SETUP: Create Code Ocean account, create new capsule, upload app files, use "environment" file to declare the code as R and load any relevant packages, click "Launch Cloud Workstation" ▶ "Shiny", publish the capsule (allows others to run it), done.
  - COST: 10 hours of free run time every month (20 GB storage) if you register with your .edu address.

---

[60] https://github.com/alan-turing-institute/the-turing-way/blob/master/workshops/boost-research-reproducibility-binder/workshop-presentations/zero-to-binder-r.md

[61] https://mybinder.readthedocs.io/en/latest/using/config_files.html

[62] `runtime.txt` + `install.R` is easiest for beginners, but there are other possibilities. See https://inundata.org/talks/rstd19/#/0/31 for an overview, and https://mybinder. readthedocs.io/en/latest/using/config_files.html for a few more details. The `holepunch` package (https://github.com/karthik/holepunch) can expedite matters, but is a work in progress.

[63] The Binder URL should end with `?urlpath=shiny/` (ending slash can matter; it hurts nothing to include it regardless) to launch the repo's R code immediately as a Shiny app. If your app's main R files live in a subfolder within the repo, the ending bit should read `?urlpath=shiny/subfolderName/`. Compiling the Binder can take a while the first time for the same reasons as fn. 65, but subsequent launches will be faster. The Binder will have to recompile any time you push a new Git commit, depending on how you constructed the Binder URL and fn. 62.

[64] https://github.com/binder-examples/r

– NOTES: App code will be visible. User must also have Code Ocean login to run the app – they will have to clone your original capsule, then run the clone. Must run app using interactive "Cloud Workstation" mode. An RStudio Cloud Workstation will require your user to do the same amount of clicking as they would if running the raw code locally. A Shiny Cloud Workstation requires your user to click a single link to launch the app. Both Cloud Workstation options require a long compile time when the app's capsule is first run (fn. 65).[65]

A.2 App Scalability

This subsection's topic is an intermediate to advanced one. If you fall into any of these groups, you can safely skip it:

- You are using a web server and your app is running into no performance issues, even when many people are using it at once.
- You are not using a server – you and/or your students are running the app locally, or you deployed your app using Docker or Electron, or you're using Binder or Code Ocean to deploy your app.

If you run into any performance issues, though, this subsection is for you. It won't explain how to improve your app's performance, but it *will* help you understand the big places where things may go awry, and where you can look for more detailed information on addressing these issues.

Shiny apps are websites (this is what R builds for you behind the scenes, using the R/Shiny code you write), which means everything we need to think about for website hosting also applies here. If you deploy your app to any web server, you will need to think about the amount of *web traffic* you expect. Ideally, you would do this before paying for anything (or before setting up and running your own Shiny server), because the app's traffic will impact how much server space, RAM, and CPU power you will need. If the number of visitors overwhelms your web server's capabilities, any Shiny app hosted on that server can crash and become temporarily inaccessible, just like any other website.

There are three relevant traffic-related questions to think about:

- How complex is the app, when it comes to the calculations it performs (and the objects it creates, and those objects' size)? [standard website question]

---

[65] The first time you launch the Cloud Workstation, it will take 2–5 minutes for all the code to compile. Complex apps will take closer to 10–20 minutes. The Workstation will also need to recompile if you modify the capsule's environment file. Subsequent runs of the Workstation will start almost immediately.

- How many people do I expect to use the app, in general? [standard website question]
- How many of those people will be using the app *at the same time*? [Shiny-specific question]

The last question is particularly important because of some R-specific details that affect Shiny. You will be affected if you plan to do an in-class activity with an app. The RStudio team talks about these R-specific details,[66] but in short: R does badly when users demand many calculations at once because it is a single-threaded process, and R receiving many calculation demands at once is exactly what happens with Shiny apps. R will eventually catch up by running each command in the order it was received. It moves only to the next backlogged command *after* the previous command finishes running entirely.

If your app's calculations finish very quickly, this backlog will be a nonissue, generally. R will work through its backlog quickly, so your users' wait time will be low. However, if you have a calculation that takes several seconds – 10000 simulation draws, perhaps – R will be tied up the entire time the calculation runs, meaning other users will be able to do NOTHING until it finishes. Crucially, that includes anything that relies on R...including **anything** for your Shiny app, even something as basic as the app loading in a browser, or switching between the app's tabs.

There are a few ways of dealing with performance problems. RStudio's article series on the topic[67] suggests working through your app's code in a specific order. You should move to the list's next item only after trying prior ones.

1. Look for places to optimize the code, in general. Check for bottlenecks, unnecessary recalculations, generating intermediate objects when you could instead use `magrittr` pipes (%>%), and/or otherwise inefficient code.
2. Tweak aspects of the web server's performance, like how it load-balances. RStudio gives a broad guide for optimizing shinyapps.io's performance.[68]
3. Use asynchronous programming (i.e., promises[69])

For further information, dive into the RStudio article links above.

---

[66] http://shiny.rstudio.com/articles/scaling-and-tuning.html
[67] https://shiny.rstudio.com/articles/#measure-usage
[68] http://shiny.rstudio.com/articles/scaling-and-tuning.html
[69] https://rstudio.github.io/promises/articles/casestudy.html

Appendix B Writing a Basic App: Predicted Quantities

In this section, I walk through creating a very basic, econometric-focused Shiny app. The idea is to help you begin (a) seeing what Shiny can do by getting your hands dirty, (b) developing your general intuition behind writing a Shiny app, and (c) specifically seeing how even small Shiny apps can make otherwise abstract econometrics concepts crisper, quicker, and less laborious to explain.

This is the only place in the Element where I go into an app's construction in detail. The main text talks only about the pedagogical motivations for each of the apps and their usefulness for reaching your pedagogical outcomes of interest.

B.1 Section's App Overview

We end up creating four separate apps in this section, all of which are heavily related.

- `predProbs` (Sect. B.3.3) [https://bit.ly/2OXScSR]: The basic app from the how-to walkthrough. It generates predicted probabilities from a logit model predicting whether a *Titanic* passenger survived the sinking.
- `predProbs` 2.0 (Sect. B.4) [http://bit.ly/2CB4smh]: Same as `predProbs`, but spiffed.
- `predProbs_HMST` (Sect. B.5) [https://bit.ly/3vK6BCN]: Same app structure as `predProbs`, but modified to allow students to replicate the predicted probability tables from an actual published article. Target table: Table 3 in Hensel, Mitchell, Sowers, and Thyne's "Bones of Contention" (2008, *Journal of Conflict Resolution*).
- `predProbsMNL` (Sect. B.6) [http://bit.ly/3g8o4fb]: Same app structure as `predProbs`, but adapted to multinomial logit. Generates predicted probabilities for Mexican voters' vote choice in the first round of the 2012 presidential election.

B.2 How Do I Start Coding with Shiny?

The heart of Shiny is creating an app that will be viewable in a web browser. What the app will do is up to you, but the underlying file architecture is the same regardless.

To begin, create a folder whose name is whatever you would like your app's name to be. A folder named "myShinyApp" would create a Shiny app named myShinyApp. There are then specific files, with specific names, that must be saved into your newly created folder. A basic Shiny app will have two such files:[70]

- `ui.R`. Creates the part of the app that the user sees and interacts with.
- `server.R`. The behind-the-scenes part of the app responsible for all the R-based calculations, returning them as objects to be referenced by `ui.R`.

From here, creating a Shiny app is a matter of learning the basics. **Shiny plays by the same rules as all R code**, but has some extra bits that make its interactive functionality possible. Many excellent tutorials already exist when it comes to building a basic Shiny app.

- RStudio has a set of video[71] and written[72] tutorials. The written tutorials cover Shiny's fundamentals well enough to get up and running. The videos provide the same with more details and elaboration. RStudio also has links to past Shiny conference talks and other tutorial resources on its main tutorial page,[73] and its article[74] series covers more intermediate- to advanced-level topics.
- For more tutorial material, the curated list[75] at Awesome R-Shiny is very extensive and has material pitched at all levels.
- Outside of the RStudio team, Dean Attali is arguably the foremost expert in Shiny, making his tutorial worth looking at.[76] Attali also has a Shiny Data-Camp course,[77] but it is a premium course, meaning only the first chapter is free to view.[78]
- DataCamp's premium[79] introductory Shiny course, titled "Building Web Applications in R with Shiny."
- Colin Fay (coauthor of the `golem` package), Sébastien Rochette, Vincent Guyader, and Cervan Girard have a book in progress[80] discussing the *process*

---

[70] It is possible for both files to be combined into one, but for complex apps, it helps organizationally to keep the files separate.

[71] https://shiny.rstudio.com/tutorial/#video-tutorials

[72] https://shiny.rstudio.com/tutorial/#written-tutorials

[73] https://shiny.rstudio.com/tutorial/

[74] https://shiny.rstudio.com/articles

[75] https://github.com/grabear/awesome-rshiny#tutorials

[76] Attali's tutorial is also one of the links in the Awesome R-shiny list. https://deanattali.com/blog/building-shiny-apps-tutorial/

[77] https://www.datacamp.com/courses/building-web-applications-in-r-with-shiny-case-studies

[78] DataCamp has a special for educators geared toward student use: you can sign up your class (https://www.datacamp.com/groups/education/) for 6 months of free access to DataCamp's entire course curriculum, including the premium courses.

[79] https://www.datacamp.com/courses/building-web-applications-with-shiny-in-r

[80] https://engineering-shiny.org/

of building Shiny apps, particularly large apps with "several thousand lines of code." The book assumes the reader can already create smaller Shiny apps.

If you want to get the most out of this section's walkthrough, I suggest you stop and do one of two things now (if not both):

- Watch sections 1–16 of RStudio's "How to Start Shiny" video tutorials.[81]
  🕐 1 hour, 16 minutes

- Read (and work) through lessons 1–6 in RStudio's seven-lesson written tutorial.[82]
  🕐 ~2 hours (based on RStudio's estimates)

What follows should not be viewed as a substitute for those tutorials and other how-to material above. You should view it as a complement. I also assume your R fundamentals are solid from this point on.

Ensure you have installed `shiny` and can run it successfully before continuing. Refer to the instructions in Appendix B.2 as needed.

I indicate code chunks using `typeset font`, indented from the surrounding text. Contents of entire files are offset in shaded boxes with syntax highlighting (see example below).

```
─────────────────────────── fileName.R ───────────────────────────
# An example of how a file's entire contents will appear, with the file's name at the
↪  code block's top and bottom
# ↪ = wrapped lines (the wrap arrow, like the one in the previous line = not character
↪  to be typed)
─────────────────────────── fileName.R ───────────────────────────
```

As a final but important aside: **indents, spaces, and line breaks in Shiny apps follow the same rules as regular R.**

- Any indentation pattern is legal. It only serves to make the code more readable to humans.
- COROLLARY: Whether you separate a function's arguments with one or more spaces is irrelevant. To R, `server <- function(input, output, session)` is equivalent to `server<-function(input,output,session)`.
- A single function's code can span multiple lines if R is still waiting for additional arguments (or a closing parenthesis or bracket) to make the function call valid.

Shiny apps end up having many nested functions, particularly in `ui.R`. You shouldn't hesitate to use indents and multiline functions liberally to keep things organized.

---

[81] https://shiny.rstudio.com/tutorial/#video-tutorials
[82] https://shiny.rstudio.com/tutorial/#written-tutorials

B.3 Writing the App: `predProbs` [https://bit.ly/2OXScSR]

B.3.1 Motivation

I do a great deal of handwaving when it comes to logit's predicted quantities in my nonmethods undergraduate classes. Most students can compute predicted quantities for linear models because $y = mx + b$ is covered thoroughly in secondary school. However, the jump to nonlinearity, in conjunction with a noncontinuous dependent variable, all in the context of a substantive class with no guaranteed methods prerequisite, is understandably a bridge too far for some. If students could *see* the longhand math for the predicted quantities, though, the calculation would likely be much less mysterious to a good swath of them.

We'll be creating a simple app named `predProbs` to show the longhand math for predicted quantities out of an estimated logit model (= predicted probabilities). Our data and model will be simple to allow us to see the app's logic more clearly. We will use the *Titanic* survival data to predict whether a passenger survived the sinking based on his/her (a) ticket type (1st Class, 2nd Class, 3rd Class), (b) age (in years), and (c) gender (female, male). Our final basic app will look like Figure B.1's screenshot.

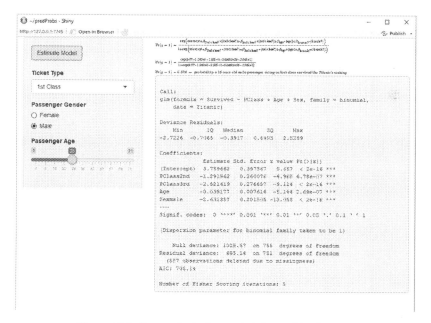

Figure B.1 Screenshot of completed `predProbs` app.
Package version: `shiny_1.3.2`

B.3.2 Planning

To create this app, it helps to start by thinking about three things. They are the same things you should think about when planning code in any language (especially when coding functions):

1. *Input.* The information you want the user to input. What the user enters will in turn affect what comes out of the app. This info can be any number[83] of things ("widgets," in Shiny speak), as Appendix B.2's resources cover. This user interactivity is what gives Shiny its power.
2. *Output.* What you want the app to do, in response to the user's input.
3. *Static.* The additional information the app will need to compute the output you want. Examples can include datasets, the type of regression model, the model's specification, the number of simulation draws, and so on.
   > NOTE: Any information you code as static could *also* be coded as inputtable by the user. Regular R functions make no distinction between these two possibilities because regular R is incapable of this type of user interactivity. R's help files collectively call them "Arguments."

Whether you code something as static or inputtable by the user depends on how complex you want the app to be. Occam's Razor is a good general rule of thumb. Focus on the app doing a few things well, with those "few things" likely relating to the app's pedagogical objective.

For this particular app, we'll be structuring things this way:

Box B.1 `predProbs`: Necessary Components to Run

Input

1. A button that, when clicked, estimates a logit model with a predefined specification
2. Covariate values

---

[83] https://shiny.rstudio.com/gallery/widget-gallery.html

Box B.1 *Continued*

Output

1. The `summary()` information from the logit model
2. Logit functional form expression that automatically updates with *both* (1) the user-selected covariate values and (2) the estimated logit coefficients
3. Computed predicted probability value

Static

1. Dataset for analysis (*Titanic* survival data from `Stat2Data` package)
2. Estimated logit model's specification (`glm(Survived ~ PClass + Age + Sex, family=binomial, data=Titanic)`)

We also could have added any static explanatory text, equations, images, videos, and so on to the "Static" list above, since you can include such information in any app. However, none of it is **required** for the app to run, which the focus of our I/O/S breakdown.

This basic example will demonstrate a few fundamental Shiny concepts that are particularly helpful when creating econometric-related apps:

Box B.2 Basic Shiny Concepts

- Using buttons to "begin" the app's calculations
- Using three different widget types for numerical input:
  - Drop-down box (for ticket type)
  - Radio buttons (for gender)
  - Slider (for age)
- Displaying LaTeX equations in the app window
- Printing text output to the app window
- Displaying text (equations, in this case) where parts of the text dynamically update, depending on what the user enters as input ("reactivity," in Shiny speak)

Finally, you will need some additional packages installed on your computer. These are the same packages you would load in R if you were doing the analysis locally (e.g., loading `ggplot2` to create `ggplot`s). Some of the packages may also be Shiny specific, to enable certain functionality. For example, `shinyBS` can display pop-up boxes, styled in a particular way.

Often, you won't know what the app's package list will look like until the entire app is finished. You will typically build the list as you go, loading what you need to accomplish a given coding task, just as you would for regular R code. We have the full package list now, since this is a worked example; none happen to be Shiny specific. Ensure they are installed on your computer.

Box B.3 `predProbs`: **Package List**

- `Stat2Data`

Because Shiny plays by the same rules as regular R, you will need `library()` statements to load any package-specific functionality you use in a given R file. In our case, with the two-file setup we'll be using, those files will be `ui.R` or `server.R`. If you use a package's functions in one of the files, but not the other, you only need to load the package in the one "using" file.[84]

B.3.3 Writing the App

We'll be managing our own file structures for this app, since its structure is so basic.

Step 1: In a location of your choosing, create a directory named "predProbs." Our app's name will then be `predProbs`.

Step 2: Inside the "predProbs" folder, create two new R files: one named `ui.R` and one named `server.R`.[85]

Step 3: Start R/RStudio, if you haven't already.

Step 4: Set your working directory to the "predProbs" folder.
To view what your Shiny app looks like at this juncture (which you can do at any point from here on, when you'd like to see how things look), you can type:

`shiny::runApp()`

---

[84] If your app eventually uses an optional `global.R` file (Sect. 2.1.3), you can place all the `library()` statements there.

[85] You can also automate these first two steps in RStudio by going File ▶ New File ▶ Shiny Web App.

Figure B.2 Screenshot of first run.
Package version: `shiny_1.3.2`

The app will then run...with an error that looks like Figure B.2.[86] The error is completely expected. There is nothing in the `ui.R` file yet (and nothing in the other places where UI information could be stored), so R is throwing up its hands in exasperation.

Step 5: Open `server.R` in R/RStudio and paste the following barebones code.

```
                                ─── server.R ───
library(Stat2Data) # to save us time later—has our example dataset

server <- function(input, output, session) {
  # All of the backend magic will go here.
}
                                ─── server.R ───
```

Save the file. This code allows the app to run while we address its appearance.

Step 6: Open `ui.R` in R/RStudio. UI stands for "user interface," so it's unsurprising this file will contain all the information `shiny` needs to display your app to the user: instructions about which widgets to display for the user to enter the information you want, instructions about where to display the app's output, and instructions about both the presence and placement of any other static information like text, equations, or images.

We haven't worried about the app's layout because `shiny` comes with a whole host of layout options, built initially from Bootstrap 2 and

---

[86] You'll need to close the app's display window manually or kill the app from the console before it will accept input again. The latter applies even if the app crashes with an error.

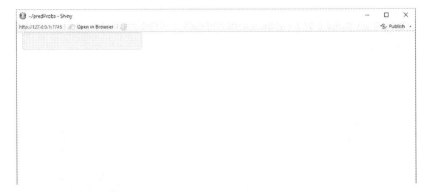

Figure B.3 Screenshot of app with UI outlined. Notice the shaded box on the left, representing the (currently empty) left sidebar. Package version: `shiny_1.3.2`

updated to more recent Bootstrap versions since.[87] Some examples of the various layouts are here.[88]

We'll use a simple, but functional, layout: an app with a small sidebar on the left and the main content on the right. There are additional R packages that provide more canned layouts of varying complexity.

To use this layout, insert the following code into `ui.R`.

```
————————————————————————— ui.R ——————————————————
ui <- fluidPage(
    sidebarLayout(
        # Define left sidebar's contents
        sidebarPanel(
            # Left sidebar's contents will go here.
        ),
        # Define main frame's contents
        mainPanel(
            # Main frame's contents will go here.
        )
    )
)
————————————————————————— ui.R ——————————————————
```
Save `ui.R`.

This gives us the barebones outline for the app's appearance. If you successfully followed the previous two steps, you should see something like Figure B.3 when you run the app.

Step 7: In `ui.R`, add the input widgets inside the `sidebarPanel` segment. If you need to, refer back to the "Input" segment in the app's I/O/S

[87] https://getbootstrap.com/2.3.2/
[88] https://shiny.rstudio.com/articles/layout-guide.html

summary box to remember what inputs we'll need. There will be four input widgets: the "Estimate Model" action button to estimate the logit, plus the three widgets for setting the covariate values.

Which type of widgets we use to gather the information we need is up to us. The order in which the widgets appear is also up to us. Where they appear in the app is up to us, too – they can go anywhere inside `fluidPage()`, or whatever your UI layout's very first argument happens to be.

Going in the order I've elected to arrange the widgets in the sidebar (while remembering this walkthrough is no substitute for going through Appendix B.2's basic tutorial material):

1. The action button to estimate the logit. We'll put this at the top to imply the user should click it first.

   ```
   actionButton("estmButton," "Estimate Model")
   ```

   There's no `shiny` syntax rule prohibiting the logit from estimating automatically when the app loads. In apps involving regressions, I like using the button for both pedagogical and practical reasons. Pedagogically, it increases students' ownership over what the app's doing, if only in the form of marginally increased awareness. Practically, the button prevents the regression from immediately reestimating, which will occur by default (for reactivity reasons) anytime the user interacts with a widget that affects information used by the regression.

2. A drop-down box for the ticket type.

   ```
   selectInput("coeffClass," "Ticket Type,"
               choices = list("1st Class" = 1, "2nd Class" = 2,
               "3rd Class" = 3), selected = 1, multiple = FALSE)
   ```

3. A set of radio buttons for gender.

   ```
   radioButtons("coeffGender," label = "Passenger Gender,"
                choices = list("Female" = 0, "Male" = 1),
                selected = 1)
   ```

4. A slider for age.

   ```
   sliderInput("coeffAge," label = "Passenger Age,"
               min = 1, max = 71, step = 1, value = 28)
   ```

   Here, we've set the slider's range to be age's lowest and highest observed values in the dataset. We could choose whatever values we like, from a code standpoint. Whether the values are substantively sensible is another matter.

   Further, we could have the app calculate age's minimum and maximum value from the dataset, rounded up to the nearest integer when needed, and insert those as the slider's start and end values. We've hardcoded the slider's range for simplicity. Same for the slider's starting value – we've arbitrarily set it to age's median, but the app could have also calculated the median for us and inserted it into the UI code.

Once we enter all the code correctly for this step, ui.R should look like this. We've optionally added two line breaks below the button (br(),br(),, equivalent to

 in HTML), as a quick way to create some separation between the button and the other input widgets:

```
─────────────────────────────── ui.R ───────────────────────────────
ui <- fluidPage(
  sidebarLayout(
    # Define left sidebar's contents
    sidebarPanel(
      # Left sidebar's contents.
      actionButton("estmButton," "Estimate Model"),
      br(),br(),       # to force some space between button and other widgets
      selectInput("coeffClass," "Ticket Type,"
                  choices = list("1st Class" = 1, "2nd Class" = 2,
                    "3rd Class" = 3), selected = 1, multiple = FALSE),
      radioButtons("coeffGender," label = "Passenger Gender,"
                   choices = list("Female" = 0, "Male" = 1),
                   selected = 1),
      sliderInput("coeffAge," label = "Passenger Age,"
                  min = 1, max = 71, step = 1, value = 28)
    ),
    # Define main frame's contents
    mainPanel(
      # Main frame's contents will go here.
    )
  )
)
─────────────────────────────── ui.R ───────────────────────────────
```

Save the file.

If you run the app, it will look like Figure B.4.

You are welcome to interact with the widgets, but nothing will occur yet. We've yet to tell R what to do when the user changes a widget's value. Those instructions are what we'll define in server.R.

From a code-syntax perspective, notice the required trailing commas for all of ui.R's code lines except the last within each nested level. As for why: take a step back and look at the code's syntax from an R perspective. Each of the lines we enter inside the ui object is (eventually) a function argument for fluidPage. And, as we know from regular R, all function arguments are separated by commas.

If you're having trouble seeing the function formatting, keep in mind that we've indented the lines for human readability. R would have no problem with the first four noncommented lines reading: ui <- fluidPage(sidebarLayout(sidebarPanel(selectInput("coeff

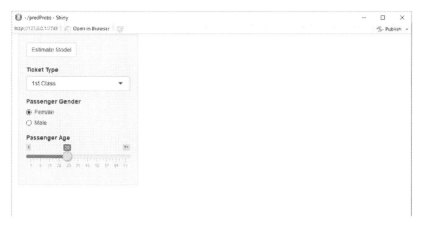

Figure B.4 Screenshot of app with completed UI input widgets in left sidebar. Package version: `shiny_1.3.2`

Class," "Ticket Type," .... The function formatting is now more obvious. Moving from right to left: `selectInput("coeff Class"...)` is the first argument of `sidebarPanel()`, which is itself the first argument of `sidebarLayout()`, which is itself the first argument of `fluidPage()`.

Step 8: NOTE: Things will start getting progressively more confusing from here out if you haven't looked at any of Appendix B.2's material.

We now have to write *all* the app's calculations. These occur in `server.R`. If `ui.R` is putting on the show on the proverbial stage, `server.R` represents the work going on behind the scenes to make that show possible.

With a very small number of exceptions, all calculations must be carried out in `server.R`. This is *always* true for all calculations involving information entered by the user, like widget values. The calculations will react dynamically to the user's input, unless we specifically tell R to behave otherwise. For any static content with no elaborate calculations, such as text explaining how to use the app, we can define it later in `ui.R`.

For our example here, we have three major calculations involving user inputs in some way: (1) estimating the logit (once the user clicks the "Estimate Model" button), (2) writing the longhand expression for the predicted probability calculation with both the values inputted by the user and the estimated logit coefficients inserted, and (3) calculating the actual predicted probability using the same information as (2). We will need to define each of these in `server.R`.

`server.R`'s contents may look strange, at first. The entire file will be filled with various function definitions. None (or very little) of the code will execute linearly to produce the behavior we expect based on the code's ordering, as we're accustomed to in regular R files (and ui.R). The code's execution will jump around, depending on the functions you define and how each is connected with ui.R.

If you understood nothing of the previous paragraph, the two key points are:

1. server.R's code will be very modular, almost entirely composed of function definitions.

2. **Just because you define the functions in a specific order does NOT mean server.R executes them in that order when the app runs.**[89] Starting to get your mind around this now will save you a lot of misery and frustration in the longer term.

Because code order doesn't affect the order in which server.R calls the various functions (execution order), you can organize server.R's code however you like. That said, it helps to either (a) go in the order you *think* the various functions will need to execute or (b) group like functions together under similar commented headers, to keep both the code and yourself organized. To reiterate, though: writing the code in rough execution order has ZERO impact on the order in which it actually executes. It is only an aesthetic convenience to help us, the humans, out.

While some of the server.R code is Shiny specific, a great deal of it should look familiar to R users. This goes back to one of the Element's unofficial secondary meta-points: writing Shiny apps involves much of the R knowledge that researchers already have.

1. Run the logit, but only when the action button is pushed.

```
results <- eventReactive(input$estmButton, {
        data(Titanic)
        glm(Survived ~ PClass + Age + Sex, family=binomial, data=Titanic)
        })
```

The curly brackets for the eventReactive function's second argument mean "run everything inside these when the first argument changes value." (You can pass in curly-bracketed arguments to regular R functions, too.) input$estmButton is an action button, and action buttons will only change in value when clicked.

---

[89] Technically, when you run the app, server.R does indeed run from start to finish (compile order). However, because the file has only function definitions, the code's first run simply means the functions are now objects in memory, available to be called by other code. The behavior's identical to what happens when you have regular R files containing only function definitions. server.R's execution order is subsequently nonlinear because how and when the functions are then used defines the code's execution order.

2. Print out the longhand mathematical equation for the predicted probability. To achieve this functionality, we'll use MathJax – a JavaScript library that permits equations to be typeset in LATEX form on a website and be scaled appropriately based on the window's size and/or any other surrounding text.

MathJax's syntax is similar to LATEX's, with many of the same rules and conventions. The MathJax team keeps an official list of TEX commands[90] supported by MathJax. The StackExchange community has also compiled a very good reference guide[91] with practical MathJax basics and other essentials.

Only one of our longhand mathematical equations will have dynamic content – the equation where we insert the user-set covariate values and estimated coefficients. That means we only need to write this equation's expression in `server.R`.

```
output$fFormExpr <- renderUI({
    # To get ticket type dummy variables set correctly
    if(input$coeffClass=="1"){
        c12 <- 0
        c13 <- 0
    } else if(input$coeffClass=="2"){
        c12 <- 1
        c13 <- 0
    } else{
        c12 <- 0
        c13 <- 1
    }

    linCombCalc <- paste0(signif(coef(results())[1],4),
                    ifelse(coef(results())[2]>=0, "+"," ""),
                        signif(coef(results())[2], 4), "*," c12,
                    ifelse(coef(results())[3]>=0, "+"," ""),
                        signif(coef(results())[3], 4), "*," c13,
                    ifelse(coef(results())[4]>=0, "+"," ""),
                        signif(coef(results())[4], 4), "*," input$coeffAge,
                    ifelse(coef(results())[5]>=0, "+"," ""),
                        signif(coef(results())[5], 4), "*," input$coeffGender
                    )
    withMathJax(
        paste(
            '\\(\\Pr(y = 1) = \\frac{\\exp \\left(', linCombCalc,'\\right)}
                        {1 + \\exp \\left(', linCombCalc,'\\right)} \\)'
        )
    )
})
```

Because we want to (eventually) print this equation in the UI window for our users to see, we wrapped the expression in a `renderUI()` call here. (Remember, for the last time: none of this is a substitute for Appendix B.2!)

We also helped ourselves out with some optional code.

90 http://docs.mathjax.org/en/latest/tex.html#tex-commands
91 https://math.meta.stackexchange.com/questions/5020/mathjax-basic-tutorial-and-quick-reference

- We broke the code into more readable chunks by defining an object with the linear index's MathJax code (`linCombCalc`) and then pasting that object into the final expression twice.
- We improved the final printed equation's readability with the `ifelse()`s. `ifelse(`*coefficient*`>=0, "+," "")` prints the appropriate sign for the coefficient indicated in the `ifelse`'s first argument. Without this code, if we separated all terms with $+$s, our final printed equation would have $+-$ printed in front of any negatively signed coefficient.
- We further improved the equation's future readability by rounding the coefficients. R will now only print the first four significant digits for each coefficient (`signif(`*value*`,4)`).

One of the things we didn't do, but could have, pertains to `server.R`'s code and its readability. For one example, we call `coef(results())` directly to access the estimated logit coefficient values. Instead, we could have created an intermediate object with a shorter name. If we had done something like:

```
betas <- coef(results())
```

the first few lines of `linCombCalc` would then read:

```
linCombCalc <- paste0(signif(betas[1],4),
                ifelse(betas[2]>=0, "+," ""),
                signif(betas[2], 4), "*," cl2, ...
```

There's no `shiny`-based reason for using (or not using) intermediate objects. The same rationale behind when and why you'd use them in regular R still applies. We didn't use intermediate objects here for two reasons: (a) to help reinforce what reactive functions do by referring to such a function (multiple times), and (b) to reduce the number of intermediate objects in memory.

a. Calculate the actual predicted probability from the estimated model, using the covariate values selected by the user via the input widgets.

```
output$predPr <- renderUI({
    # To get ticket type dummy variables set correctly
    if(input$coeffClass=="1"){
        cl2 <- 0
        cl3 <- 0
    } else if(input$coeffClass=="2"){
        cl2 <- 1
        cl3 <- 0
    } else{
        cl2 <- 0
        cl3 <- 1
    }

    val <- plogis(
            coef(results())[1] + coef(results())[2]*cl2 +
            coef(results())[3]*cl3 + coef(results())[4]*input$coeffAge +
            coef(results())[5]*as.numeric(input$coeffGender)
            )
```

```
withMathJax(
  paste0(
    '\\(\\\Pr(y = 1) = ', signif(val,3),
      ' \\Leftarrow \\text{ probability a ', input$coeffAge, '-year-old ',
      ifelse(as.numeric(input$coeffGender)==0, "female," "male"),
      ' passenger riding in ',
      ifelse(input$coeffClass=="1," "first class,"
        ifelse(input$coeffClass=="2," "second class," "third class")
      ), ' survived the } \\mathit{Titanic} \\text{\'s sinking}\\)'
    )
  )
})
```

We opted to print the predicted probability value using MathJax, to make all the mathematical expressions have the same styling. We could have just as easily used `renderText()`, Shiny's version of `print()`, to return a printed number. It's purely a matter of preference.

A few things to note here. First, we added a substantive prose description in MathJax of what the quantity's telling us about our substantive question – what's the probability that a passenger with these characteristics got off the ship alive? (Code starting with `\\Leftarrow`)

Second, we used R's canned `plogis()` function. We could have instead used logit's actual mathematical expression $\frac{\exp(XB)}{1+\exp(XB)}$ for the calculation. We used the function merely to demonstrate such a thing can still be done, same as regular R.

Third, you'll notice we repeat one of `output$fFormExp`'s code chunks (`if(input$coeffClass=="1"){ ...}`). We could eliminate the repetition by defining a third function to pull and store the covariate values for ticket type, and then call that function in `output$fFormExp` and here in `output$predPr` to get ticket type's covariate values. We opted not to do so here for simplicity and straightforwardness.

Fourth and finally, we also used two separate objects to hold the functional form expression and actual predicted probability value. MathJax does allow you to write them as a single object, with line breaks denoted `////`. If you do this, you can even align the two equations on their equal signs, same as you can in LaTeX. We wrote them as two simple objects here for the same reasons as above: simplicity and straightforwardness.

Step 9: To finish up in `server.R`, we need to add a function to print the model summary to the UI window. (Recall Appendix B.2's material: if we want to display any of `server.R`'s calculations in `ui.R`, we need to wrap the calculation's output in an appropriate `render*()` function within `server.R`.)

To keep things simple, we'll print the output from `summary()` verbatim. However, we could create a more visually appealing coefficient table, if we wanted.

```
output$modObj <- renderPrint({
                    summary(results())
              })
```

Save the file.

After inserting the code from this step and the previous one, your `server.R` file should look like this. If you run the app at this point, there'll be no visible difference from Figure B.4 (which makes sense – we made no changes to `ui.R`, the file responsible for the app's appearance):

```
─────────────────────── server.R ───────────────────────
library(Stat2Data)

server <- function(input, output, session){
    results <- eventReactive(input$estmButton, {
                data(Titanic)
                glm(Survived ~ PClass + Age + Sex, family=binomial, data=Titanic)
            })

    output$modObj <- renderPrint({
                    summary(results())
                })

    output$fFormExpr <- renderUI({
        # To get ticket type dummy variables set correctly
        if(input$coeffClass=="1"){
            cl2 <- 0
            cl3 <- 0
        } else if(input$coeffClass=="2"){
            cl2 <- 1
            cl3 <- 0
        } else{
            cl2 <- 0
            cl3 <- 1
        }

        linCombCalc <- paste0(signif(coef(results())[1],4),
                            ifelse(coef(results())[2]>=0, "+," ""),
                                signif(coef(results())[2], 4), "*," cl2,
                            ifelse(coef(results())[3]>=0, "+," ""),
                                signif(coef(results())[3], 4), "*," cl3,
                            ifelse(coef(results())[4]>=0, "+," ""),
                                signif(coef(results())[4], 4), "*,"
                                ↳ input$coeffAge,
                            ifelse(coef(results())[5]>=0, "+," ""),
                                signif(coef(results())[5], 4), "*,"
                                ↳ input$coeffGender
                        )
```

```
    withMathJax(
        paste(
            '\\(\\Pr(y = 1) = \\frac{\\exp \\left(', linCombCalc,'\\right)}
                {1 + \\exp \\left(', linCombCalc,'\\right)} \\)'
        )
    )
})


output$predPr <- renderUI({
    # To get ticket type dummy variables set correctly
    if(input$coeffClass=="1"){
        cl2 <- 0
        cl3 <- 0
    } else if(input$coeffClass=="2"){
        cl2 <- 1
        cl3 <- 0
    } else{
        cl2 <- 0
        cl3 <- 1
    }

    val <- plogis(
            coef(results())[1] + coef(results())[2]*cl2 +
            coef(results())[3]*cl3 + coef(results())[4]*input$coeffAge +
            coef(results())[5]*as.numeric(input$coeffGender)
        )

    withMathJax(

        paste0(
            '\\(\\Pr(y = 1) = ', signif(val,3), ' \\Leftarrow \\text{
            ↪ probability a ', input$coeffAge, '-year-old ',
            ↪ ifelse(as.numeric(input$coeffGender)==0, "female," "male"), '
            ↪ passenger riding in ', ifelse(input$coeffClass=="1," "first
            ↪ class," ifelse(input$coeffClass=="2," "second class," "third
            ↪ class")), ' survived the } \\mathit{Titanic} \\text{\'s
            ↪ sinking}\\)'
        )
    )
})
}
```
————————————————————————— server.R —————————————————————————

We'll be making no additions to `server.R` – all our work here is complete. However, that's unusual. There's typically a great deal of switching back and forth between the UI and server files as you write an app, especially for more complex apps with multiple parts.

Step 10: Switch back to `ui.R`. We can now fill in the main frame's content. We'll take care of the static information first. By "static," we mean information that's the same, regardless of the input widgets' values. Usually, it's text, but we aren't limited only to that. In our case, we wanted to write out logit's generic predicted probability formula before we substituted in numerical values.

We'll again be using MathJax to write the expression. Inside the `mainPanel` chunk, insert the following:

```
withMathJax(), # enables the display of MathJax equations in the UI
p(
  '\\(\\Pr(y = 1) = \\frac{\\exp \\left(
      \\text{intercept} + \\beta_\\text{2nd class?}*\\left( \\text{2nd class?}
      \\right)
      + \\beta_\\text{3rd class?}*\\left( \\text{3rd class?} \\right)
      + \\beta_\\text{age}*\\left( \\text{age} \\right)
      + \\beta_\\text{male?}*\\left( \\text{male?} \\right)
     \\right)}{1 + \\exp \\left(
      \\text{intercept} + \\beta_\\text{2nd class?}*\\left( \\text{2nd class?}
      \\right)
      + \\beta_\\text{3rd class?}*\\left( \\text{3rd class?} \\right)
      + \\beta_\\text{age}*\\left( \\text{age} \\right)
      + \\beta_\\text{male?}*\\left( \\text{male?} \\right)
    \\right)} \\)'
)
```

`p()` is the equivalent of HTML's `<p>`. Wrapping the MathJax statement in `p()` is optional, but a good habit to get into, in line with best practices for coding websites.[92]

If you run the app now, you should see something like Figure B.5.

As a brief aside, MathJax expressions can sometimes have odd scaling in the R Shiny app window, affecting its legibility. There are two fixes:

- Right click on the expression and adjust the "Math Settings" options. Your settings won't persist after you close the app window, so you'll have to reset them repeatedly.
- Select "Open in Browser" to see what the app will look like in a web browser. The scaling issue should be fixed. If not, adjust the MathJax options from the previous bullet.

If the equation doesn't render in both the app's pop-up window and a browser, make sure MathJax displays on your computer. Point your browser to RStudio's example MathJax app.[93] If the equations don't render, you need to figure out why your *computer* isn't displaying MathJax. (Check a few different browsers to help with the troubleshooting.) If the equations do render in RStudio's MathJax app, you've made a mistake somewhere in a MathJax expression within `predProbs`.

Step 11: Finally, we need to print all the dynamic information we calculated in `server.R` back to `ui.R` so the user can see it. Returning to the theater

---

[92] If you do, you also have the option of styling all the paragraph text using CSS. This is a more advanced option, though, and not required for the app to run.

[93] https://shiny.rstudio.com/gallery/mathjax.html

Figure B.5 Screenshot of app with static functional form expression in UI's main frame.
Package version: shiny_1.3.2

analogy: all the show's set pieces are now complete, but still sitting backstage. In order for the audience to see any of them, we need to move them on stage.

We already made this task possible by declaring output$___ objects in server.R. These objects will be valid to display in ui.R because of the respective render*() functions we used to define them. Consider each output$___ object's existence to be the equivalent of saying "there are now stagehands around, ready to move this specific piece to the main stage, on your say-so."

We need to pass three things from server.R to ui.R. By inserting the following statements into ui.R, you're telling Shiny "move this on to the stage NOW." *All* ui.R code receiving output from server.R must be wrapped in a *Output() call.

1. The predicted probability longhand expression with the coefficient and covariate values inserted.

    uiOutput("fFormExpr")

2. The calculated predicted probability value.

    uiOutput("predPr")

3. The output from summary().

    verbatimTextOutput("modObj")

Insert these statements underneath the generic predicted probability code from the previous step, which will make them appear under that equation. Add trailing commas where appropriate to separate the various *Output() functions. Once you do, your ui.R should look like this:

```r
                                      ui.R
ui <- fluidPage(
  sidebarLayout(
    # Define left sidebar's contents
    sidebarPanel(
      # Left sidebar's contents.
      actionButton("estmButton," "Estimate Model"),
      br(),br(),        # to force some space between button and other widgets
      selectInput("coeffClass," "Ticket Type,"
                  choices = list("1st Class" = 1, "2nd Class" = 2, "3rd Class" =
                  ↪  3),
                  selected = 1, multiple = FALSE),
           radioButtons("coeffGender," label = "Passenger Gender,"
                        choices = list("Female" = 0, "Male" = 1),
                        selected = 1),
         sliderInput("coeffAge," label = "Passenger Age,"
                     min = 1, max = 71, step = 1, value = 28)
    ),
    # Define main frame's contents
    mainPanel(
      # Main frame's contents
      withMathJax(),
      p(
        '\\(\\(\\Pr(y = 1) = \\frac{\\exp \\left(
          \\text{intercept} + \\beta_\\text{2nd class?}*\\left( \\text{2nd
  ↪  class?} \\right)
          + \\beta_\\text{3rd class?}*\\left( \\text{3rd class?} \\right)
          + \\beta_\\text{age}*\\left( \\text{age} \\right)
          + \\beta_\\text{male?}*\\left( \\text{male?} \\right)
          \\right)}{1 + \\exp \\left(
          \\text{intercept} + \\beta_\\text{2nd class?}*\\left( \\text{2nd
  ↪  class?} \\right)
          + \\beta_\\text{3rd class?}*\\left( \\text{3rd class?} \\right)
          + \\beta_\\text{age}*\\left( \\text{age} \\right)
          + \\beta_\\text{male?}*\\left( \\text{male?} \\right)
          \\right)} \\)'
      ),
      uiOutput("fFormExpr"),
      uiOutput("predPr"),
      verbatimTextOutput("modObj")
    )
  )
)
                                      ui.R
```

Run the app. When the app first loads, what you see should be identical to Figure B.5. However, once you click "Estimate Model," you should see something like Figure B.1. The two nonstatic predicted probability expressions should update when you move the input widgets.

Our `predProbs` app is now complete. Congratulations.

B.4 Potential Additions: `predProbs` 2.0 [http://bit.ly/2CB4smh]

`predProbs` is simple, but does its job. It helps drive two big things home to users:

- The second equation's inserted coefficient values come from the raw logit results. It also provides the familiar `summary()` output to help facilitate that connection, for users familiar with running regressions in R.
- Predicted probabilities are less complicated to calculate and interpret than it seems. The app shows this by updating three key parts of its output when the user chooses a particular covariate value:
  - The longhand expression for the predicted probability calculation (second equation)
  - The predicted probability's calculated value (last equation/expression)
  - The substantive explanation next to the predicted probability's calculated value

That said, there are a number of additions we could make to the app. The list isn't exhaustive, but covers some potentially desirable functionality. We've already mentioned some of it in passing while writing the app:

- We didn't modify the UI's visual appearance. Part 3 of RStudio's video tutorial[94] talks about the basics. The articles in the "Build" section[95] of RStudio's more advanced materials do as well.
- Our regression output is not aesthetically pleasing. It will also be nearly worthless for students with no R experience.
- The user can currently interact with the widgets before estimating the logit model. Doing so affects and hurts nothing, from a code perspective. Pedagogically, though, we might want to seize the opportunity to reinforce that *no predicted quantities are calculable until you estimate a regression model*, perhaps by disabling the covariate value widgets until the model is estimated.
- We haven't provided any static text: there is no title, headers, or any other sort of explanatory text, including basic paragraphs.

Version 2.0 of the app addresses these four things (Figures B.6a, B.6b), along with some other additions:

- PACKAGE ADDITIONS: `shinyjs`, `shinythemes`, `stargazer`

---

[94] https://shiny.rstudio.com/tutorial/#video-tutorials
[95] https://shiny.rstudio.com/articles/#user-interface

(a)   (b)

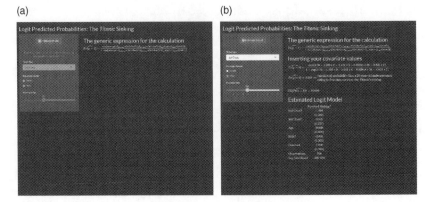

Figure B.6 predProbs 2.0
Package version: shiny_1.4.0.2

- It uses a helper function to set the covariate values for ticket type, eliminating the duplicate code.
- It puts coef(results()) into an intermediate object in multiple places within server.R, to help with code readability.
- It creates a helper function to paste in ifelse(beta>=0, "+", ""), signif(beta, 4) when needed in the MathJax equations, also to help with code readability.
- It combines output$fFormExp and output$predPr into a single object with two aligned equations, output$fFormPrExp.
- It puts hats over the predicted quantities, to denote they're predictions. It also tweaks the substantive explanation to make the "predicted" part clear.
- It uses what we know about LaTeX to wrap the substantive explanation next to the predicted value.
- It acknowledges the uncertainty around the predicted probability by also displaying its standard error.
- It uses the stargazer package to produce a nicely formatted regression table instead of the raw summary() output.
- The age slider's min, max, and starting values are no longer hardcoded. predProbs2 now calculates age's min, max, and median values using the observed data, and then sets those as the slider's min, max, and starting values, respectively.
- It provides some quick explanatory text in "hidden" places. Hover your cursor over the "Inserting your covariate values" and "Estimated Logit Model" header text to see what happens. (There are more sophisticated ways of getting the same functionality, like shinyBS's bsTooltip().)

If you want additional practice creating another basic app, Dean Attali's tutorial is a good next step. Attali's tutorial app examines liquor prices in British Columbia within a user-specified price range. It also makes use of different output types than predProbs: (1) a histogram and (2) a table containing the dataset rows meeting your specified conditions.[96]

B.5 Modification: Hensel et al. Replication [https://bit.ly/3vK6BCN]

predProbs deliberately used a simple dataset, but we can use more complex datasets about social science phenomena. Here, we'll modify predProbs to allow students to replicate the predicted probability tables from a published article. Our target will be Table 3 in Hensel, Mitchell, Sowers, and Thyne (2008). In this paper, Hensel et al. (hereafter "HMST") investigate the determinants of militarized and peaceful settlement attempts in geopolitical disputes between countries (Figure B.7).

Aside from the obvious dataset change and concomitant model specification changes, our new predProbs_HMST app has some additional adjustments from predProbs 2.0:

- ui.R: Widget to select dependent variable (HMST's Table 3 has two possible DVs)
- ui.R: Extra widgets to input the additional covariates' values
- ui.R: Button to set all covariates to mean (if continuous) or median (if categorical), for convenience
- ui.R: Gives option for model output to be displayed as a formatted stargazer table, raw R output (summary()), or raw Stata output (pre-estimated elsewhere and saved)
- server.R: Use predict() to calculate the predicted probability value for a given covariate profile, to save us from typing out each term in the linear combination manually

Additionally, we will need two packages to match the printed model output with Hensel et al.'s table of model results (Table 2), as well as the Shiny-specific packages that appear in predProbs 2.0.

---

[96] https://deanattali.com/blog/building-shiny-apps-tutorial/

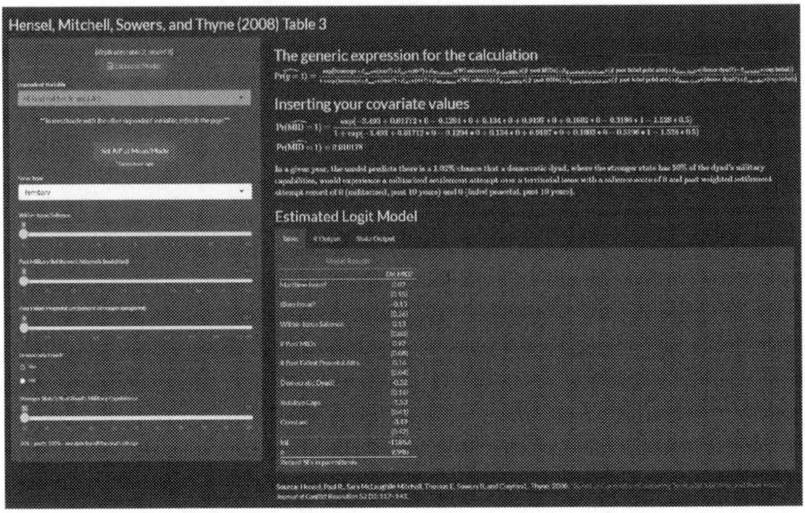

Figure B.7 Screenshot of `predProbs_HMST`.
Package version: `shiny_1.4.0.2`

Box B.4 `predProbs_HMST`: **Package List**

- `dplyr`
- `haven`
- `lmtest`
- `sandwich`
- `shinycssloaders`
- `shinyjs`
- `shinythemes`
- `shinyWidgets`
- `stargazer`

All the packages are loaded in `global.R`, an optional file that executes first when present in an app's directory. The contents of the file are accessible to both `server.R` and `ui.R`.

B.6 Extension: Multinomial Logit
(`predProbsMNL`) [`http://bit.ly/3g8o4fb`]

We can also extend the app to predicted quantities from more complex models. As an example, we'll use a multinomial logit (MNL) model to predict Mexican voters' vote choice in the first round of the 2012 presidential election (Figure B.8). `predProbs` 2.0's basic structure still works, as do some of the tweaks we

Predicted Probs: Vote Choice in the 2012 Mexican Presidential Election

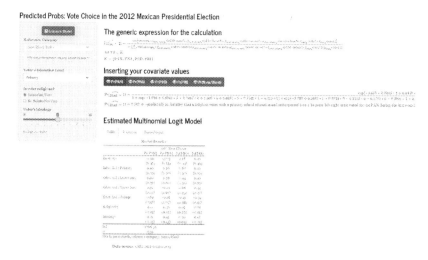

Figure B.8 Screenshot of `predProbsMNL`.
(equation continues offscreen)
Package version: `shiny_1.4.0.2`

made for `predProbs_HMST`, but we will have to make more extensive changes
to convert it into a new MNL app (`predProbsMNL`):

- `ui.R`: Changing the static functional form expression from logit to multinomial logit
- `server.R`: Changing the functional form expressions with inserted covariate values and model estimates from logit to multinomial logit
- `server.R`: Changing the calculated predicted probabilities to use multinomial logit (will also use `predict()` to expedite, same as `predProbs_HMST`)
- `ui.R`: Reconceiving how to display the calculated predicted probabilities (we will now have *K* quantities, where *K* = number of DV categories)
- `ui.R`: Adding a widget for the MNL's baseline category

Box B.5 `predProbsMNL`**: Package List**

- `dplyr`
- `haven`
- `mlogit`
- `shinycssloaders`

Box B.5 *Continued*

- shinyjs
- shinythemes
- shinyWidgets
- stargazer
- stringr

The row of buttons under "Inserting your covariate values" allow you to toggle which of the five outcomes' expressions will be visible.

References

Bahls, P. (2012). *Student Writing in the Quantitative Disciplines: A Guide for College Faculty*. San Francisco: Jossey-Bass Publishers.

Beauchamp, N. (2017). Predicting and Interpolating State-Level Polls Using Twitter Textual Data. *American Journal of Political Science 61*(2), 490–503.

Biggs, J., and C. Tang (2011). *Teaching for Quality Learning at University* (4th ed.). Maidenhead, UK: Open University Press.

Carsey, T. M., and J. J. Harden (2013). *Monte Carlo Simulation and Resampling Methods for Social Science*. Los Angeles: Sage.

Fox, J. (2016). *Applied Regression Analysis and Generalized Linear Models* (3rd ed.). Los Angeles: Sage.

Gelman, A., and D. Nolan (2017). *Teaching Statistics: A Bag of Tricks* (2nd ed.). Oxford: Oxford University Press.

Groth, R. E. (2013). *Teaching Mathematics in Grades 6–12: Developing Research-Based Instructional Practices*. Los Angeles: Sage.

Hensel, P. R., S. M. Mitchell, T. E. Sowers, and C. L. Thyne (2008). Bones of Contention: Comparing Territorial, Maritime, and River Issues. *Journal of Conflict Resolution 52*(1), 117–143.

Kennedy, P. (2003). *A Guide to Econometrics* (5th ed.). Cambridge, MA: MIT Press.

Menary, R. (2007). Writing as Thinking. *Language Sciences 29*(5), 621–632.

National Council of Teachers of Mathematics (2000). *Principles and Standards for School Mathematics*. Reston, VA: NCTM.

Yancey, K. B. (2009). Reflection and Electronic Portfolios: Inventing the Self and Reinventing the University. In D. Cambridge, B. L. Cambridge, and K. B. Yancey (eds.), *Electronic Portfolios 2.0: Emergent Research on Implementation and Impact*, pp. 5–16. Sterling, VA: Stylus Publishing.

Data Availability Statement

R scripts accompanying this Element can be run interactively online via Code Ocean. The link can be found below:

https://doi.org/10.24433/CO.2852743.v1

Cambridge Elements ⹀

Quantitative and Computational Methods for the Social Sciences

R. Michael Alvarez

California Institute of Technology

R. Michael Alvarez has taught at the California Institute of Technology his entire career, focusing on elections, voting behavior, election technology, and research methodologies. He has written or edited a number of books (recently, *Computational Social Science: Discovery and Prediction*, and *Evaluating Elections: A Handbook of Methods and Standards*) and numerous academic articles and reports.

Nathaniel Beck

New York University

Nathaniel Beck is Professor of Politics at NYU (and Affiliated Faculty at the NYU Center for Data Science) where he has been since 2003; before which he was Professor of Political Science at the University of California, San Diego. He is the founding editor of the quarterly, *Political Analysis*. He is a fellow of both the American Academy of Arts and Sciences and the Society for Political Methodology.

About the Series

The Elements Series Quantitative and Computational Methods for the Social Sciences contains short introductions and hands-on tutorials to innovative methodologies. These are often so new that they have no textbook treatment or no detailed treatment on how the method is used in practice. Among emerging areas of interest for social scientists, the series presents machine learning methods, the use of new technologies for the collection of data and new techniques for assessing causality with experimental and quasi-experimental data.

Cambridge Elements $\equiv$

Quantitative and Computational Methods for the Social Sciences

Printed in the United States
by Baker & Taylor Publisher Services